Effective
Financial
Management

A Practical Guide for School Business
Managers and Governors

A companion publication to *Effective Governance*,
also published by John Catt Educational,
in partnership with FASNA

First Published 2014
by John Catt Educational Ltd,
12 Deben Mill Business Centre, Old Maltings Approach,
Melton, Woodbridge IP12 1BL
Tel: +44 (0) 1394 389850 Fax: +44 (0) 1394 386893
Email: enquiries@johncatt.com
Website: www.johncatt.com

Opinions expressed in this publication are those of the contributors and are
not necessarily those of the publishers or the editors. We cannot accept
responsibility for any errors or omissions.

ISBN: 978 1 909717 25 1

Set and designed by John Catt Educational Limited

Printed and bound in Great Britain
by Ashford Colour Press

Foreword

Finance matters

The demands on school business managers (or more accurately those who manage the finances on behalf of the school) have become greater because of the demand for greater and more transparent accountability. However, schools business managers are not stand-alone in the process. Best practice involves joined-up leadership and accountability with Headteachers, business managers and governors aware of their responsibilities for financial probity and diligence in their management of public money.

Effective Financial Management is the companion guide to *Effective Governance*, which was published by FASNA in 2013 and has been very well received. It is a practical guide written mostly by school business managers and governors for other school business managers and governors. It is not a manual but it is a resource, case study by case study, towards understanding and sharing effective practice. Each case study describes how people at the frontline have responded to the demands made upon them by government, by Ofsted and by the Education Funding Agency. All contributors are aware that schools cannot be judged 'outstanding' unless there is effective teaching and learning, effective governance and effective management of the school budget.

Effective Financial Management can only be a contribution to supporting governors and school business managers but its strength lies in the fact that it is immensely well grounded and practical. It can be used as part of on-going professional development programmes for governors and school business managers such as those offered by FASNA.

I am delighted to recommend this guide and to celebrate the contributions from business managers and governors from a wide range of primary and secondary schools. In particular I should like to thank Joan Binder and Peter Beaven for their drive and the many, many hours spent in commissioning and editing this work - tasks in which they have been well supported by Rosaria Baldi-Adinolfi at FASNA at the proofing stage.

Tom Clark CBE, Chair, FASNA

Contents

Section 4 - Financial Procedures - The Audit Process

Section 5 - Procurement - Purchasing Supplies and Services

Section 6 - Premises and Facilities Management

Section 7 - Bid Writing including Capital Grant Projects

Section 8 - Income Generation

Section 9 - Managing Catering

Section 10 - Practicalities of Conversion for the School Business Manager

Section 11 - School Business Manager as Clerk to Governors and Company Secretary

Section 12 – 'A year in the life of'

Introduction

Peter Lauener, Chief Executive, The Education Funding Agency

The last 30 years has seen schools becoming increasingly autonomous. One of FASNA's straplines, which I particularly like, is:

FASNA believes in raising standards through Autonomy with Accountability

This should apply just as much in terms of standards of financial management as it does for pupils' achievement.

There is a huge amount of guidance and support available from organisations such as FASNA, and on-line resources including the Governors' Handbook and the Academies Financial Handbook. And I welcome this new publication as a practitioners' guide with a wealth of up to date examples from successful schools around the country.

My personal checklist of the ingredients of effective financial management would be:

- **Have the right staff** – Think about the qualifications and experience needed to deliver the finance function, dependent on the risk, scale and complexity of your financial operations
- **Plan your finances** – In addition to balancing the budgets year by year, think ahead about the financial impact of changes in pupil numbers and the maintenance and improvement of your buildings. Develop the right key performance indicators
- **Financial monitoring and reporting** – Keep your budget and assumptions up to date. Make sure financial reports for governors are clear and accessible
- **Operational controls** – Make sure you have the right day-to-day processes in place. Accounting packages need to be fit-for-purpose and kept up to date. You should have a scheme of delegation so that everyone knows their authority to spend money. And procurement should be conducted openly and transparently, avoiding conflicts of interest, and with proportionate testing of the market to demonstrate value for money. You should also manage payroll arrangements and cash flow effectively and ensure all other assets are under governors' control. And have a means of controlling risks by maintaining a risk register and drawing up contingency plans
- **Scrutiny and audit** – View these as an opportunity to discuss with governors what is working well and what needs some attention. Governors should also debate and agree how to act upon recommendations made by auditors or funding agencies such as the EFA

As you read through this guide my three key messages are:

- **Make sure everyone knows what they should do** – Understand and apply the requirements set by the law, funding bodies and your own governing documents
- **Have robust oversight** – Monitor progress and compliance and be ready to take decisive action if problems are identified
- **Aim for the best** – What can you learn from this guide that can improve what you already do?

Our experience in the Education Funding Agency is that the vast majority of schools in all sectors are well run. But in a small number of cases, financial management can go wrong, leading to excessive, improper or, in the most extreme cases, fraudulent spending. And of course any of these problems can have an adverse impact on education standards, and lead to public criticism. Effective financial management is therefore essential to help a school achieve its objectives; make effective and efficient use of resources; and sustain long-term improvement.

'A must-read'

Stephen Morales, Executive Director, NASBM

Since School Business Managers (or Bursars as they were known) emerged in the state sector in the late 80s the profession has changed immeasurably.

Increased local autonomy, more complex operations and more rigorous direct accountability mean that all schools now require highly skilled specialists to support head teachers and governors.

This guide provides the reader with a flavour of the outstanding work carried out by school business management professionals across the country.

Accountability is not always clearly understood in schools but this guide provides an excellent perspective on who is responsible and accountable for what, from the head teacher, as the accounting officer, to governors as registered directors.

Schools are complex business operations. The triangulation of effective administration, robust governance and educational leadership excellence are the key ingredients in successful schools.

This publication is a must-read for aspiring and practising School Business Managers, Headteachers and governors!

Stephen Morales, Executive Director,
National Association of School Business Managers (NASBM)

Chapter 1

The role of the school business manager

1a. Introduction

This chapter looks at the overall role of the School Business Manager (SBM) and appropriate qualifications and skills.

Focus of the chapter

This chapter will help the SBM to gain confidence to undertake their role. It will clarify for governors what they can expect from their SBM. It is intended to provide an overview of the role and not go into detail of all aspects of the role. These will be addressed in subsequent chapters.

The key questions a SBM might want to think about, and governors should ask, are:

- What are the key elements of the SBM's role?
- What is the staffing structure and how many staff does the SBM manage?
- What is the SBM's role with regard to the senior leadership team?
- What additional professional development has the SBM undertaken to help them be confident in their role?
- What professional qualifications have they obtained?
- What does the SBM like most about the job?

The key questions a SBM might want to think about, and governors should ask, in an academy are:

- What are the key elements of the SBM's role after converting to an academy?
- What are the key differences between the SBM's role in an academy and the role in the former school?
- How many staff does the SBM manage in the academy and how has this element changed since conversion?
- What additional professional development has the SBM undertaken to help them be confident in the academy setting?
- What are the best things about the new role?
- Would the SBM do it again?

Context

In this guide we are using the term School Business Manager (SBM) to cover a varied range of job descriptions and responsibilities, with the common denominator of overall responsibility for financial elements including budget preparation, monitoring, end of year accounts and liaising with governors and Headteacher as appropriate.

The government increasingly sees this role as an important part of the leadership of the school and has made a number of grants available, particularly to primary schools, in order that they can afford to have a suitably qualified and experienced person in the role. It is becoming more usual for a group of primary schools to employ a School Business Manager for the group and have a lead Finance Officer in each school to manage the day-to-day financial needs.

Overview

An important tool for the SBM is a Financial Procedures Manual which clearly sets out the systems, processes, delegated powers, authorisation limits and other responsibilities for the efficient management of the school finances. Every school should develop one of these. For academies the key document is the Academies Financial Handbook, which is issued by the Education Funding Agency. Maintained schools must comply with their local authority equivalent.

The financial procedures manual should also make explicit to other budget holders in the school exactly how they are to undertake their responsibility with regard to purchasing processes, authorisation limits and asset management and give them confidence to do so effectively to support teaching and learning.

In some schools the SBM will have a wide ranging role including leading on HR matters, overseeing the management of the premises and site, including cleaning, overseeing the catering service or leading the business development of the school perhaps through a trading company. In other settings the SBM will have a less expansive role focused mainly on financial management. This is one reason for a difference in pay from one institution to another. The more complex and all-encompassing the role, the less it can be seen as a 'nine-to-five' job.

Important qualifications and skills

There is a range of qualifications which can underpin and support the role of SBM.

- Level 4 Diploma in School Business Management, designed to provide SBMs with the skills and competences to undertake the wide range of tasks expected of them in 21st century schools
- Level 5 Diploma in School Business Management, designed to provide SBMs with the leadership skills to play an effective role in the school Senior Leadership Team (SLT)
- Level 6 Diploma in School Business Management, designed to provide SMBs with a higher level of competence to deal with more complex strategic, organisational and operational challenges
- There is also a School Business Director (SBD) programme at Master's level which marks the completion of a career pathway and which meets the diverse needs of schools, groups of schools and SMBs working in them

These qualifications are accredited by the Institute of Leadership and Management, and delivered by a number of different providers. The most experienced providers for the SBM qualifications are The SBM Partnership (made up of Serco, Adfecto and NASBM) and Anglia Ruskin.

For further details visit:

www.nasbm.co.uk/Career-Development/Qualifications-and-Development-Pathways.aspx

In addition, there are also professional accounting awards from such organisations as the Chartered Institute of Public Finance and Accountancy and the Institute of Chartered Accountants.

Some SBMs have a relevant business studies or financial services degree. There are many opportunities for professional development in this field and many very experienced SBMs have gained qualifications over a period of time.

Useful skills range from the basic to higher level skills and will vary according to the size of school, or even the group of schools (in a Multi Academy Trust for example) and whether a school is maintained or an academy. They include:

- Obvious basic skills include:
  - the ability to understand the structure of the school budget
  - monitoring cost centres
  - reporting on income and expenditure
  - maintaining accurate financial records
- Strategic and analytical skills to:
  - contribute to the identification of the school vision and school priorities
  - respond to changing demographics or new budget initiatives
  - effectively plan three and five years ahead to ensure consistency of school improvement
- Leadership skills to manage and develop a team of staff and work effectively with other senior leaders in the school
- Interpersonal skills to build relationships with governors, staff and external organisations
- Operational skills to effectively manage:
  - the school finances
  - technology, including accounting software and management information systems
  - premises including cleaning
  - and other areas such as catering
- Business development skills to enhance the school's budget through:
  - the acquisition of grants
  - utilisation of the premises
  - fundraising and/or trading
- Management of change skills as this can be an important part of the role if the HR function resides with the SBM

What of governors?

Governors should be aware of the skills required, and the skills possessed, by their SBM and the rest of the Finance Team. They should have oversight of the range of roles performed by the SBM and ensure that the breadth of the role is manageable and that the SBM possesses the skills to carry out all aspects of the role.

They should be aware of the Financial Procedures Manual and understand the procedures to be followed. It is the governors who have the ultimate responsibility of ensuring that these procedures are correct and properly followed. In an academy they will have the responsibility of appointing a Responsible Officer and an Audit Committee.

Governors should also require the Headteacher to inform them of the Performance Management of the SBM and they should have an input into that review.

And finally...

The SBM should have confidence in their ability to undertake the role effectively and efficiently. Many SBMs will say that what they enjoy most about the role is the variety of tasks, the variety from one day to the next and the knowledge that what they are doing can have a real impact on the development of the school. A good SBM has a more wide-ranging influence on the school than simply ensuring the finances are well managed. The SBM has the security of knowing that achieving 'value for money' drives decisions about the use of financial resources, releases other staff to focus more effectively on their roles, and supports the strategies to raise standards.

We hope that the following chapters and case studies will provide SBMs and governors with practical information in undertaking their roles, an insight into the variety of tasks and examples of good practice from the primary and secondary phases.

1b. Case Study – The Secondary Experience

Alison Wyatt is the Bursar at Midsomer Norton Schools Partnership. This consists of two secondary school academies in a hard Federation with over 2000 students and a combined budget of about £10 million. The Partnership is about to expand to include a local primary school.

Here Alison describes the potential breadth of the role, explains why she enjoys it and then identifies some of the main differences between community schools and academies in terms of the SBM's role. Alison is a qualified accountant although this is not a statutory requirement of the role of SBM.

Overview

There is no really appropriate model job description for a SBM. It is true to say that the role can differ considerably from institution to institution. The variables are around the type of institution and the skills and qualifications usually of an incumbent post holder on conversion to academy status. My job title is Bursar, which is used increasingly in the secondary sector to reflect a wide-ranging leadership role.

In my experience it is usual for the SBM to have responsibility for finance, premises (including catering and cleaning), Human Resources and school support staff. Other responsibilities can include, amongst others, managing a Community Sports Centre, ICT, public relations, income generation, exam data, and everyone's favourite, Health and Safety.

Usually, and as a move supported by government, the SBM is considered part of the leadership of the school. As such, they contribute at a whole school level to strategic direction and management, providing reports and presentations at governor and trustee level as and when required. The leadership role may extend across schools in more than one phase or across a group of schools in the same phase in a Multi Academy Trust or Federated structures. This reflects my current perspective. With the emphasis from government now on 'outstanding' schools 'sponsoring' less effective schools there is the potential for the role of the SBM to expand again to play an integral part of the support package across more than one school. This has all the benefits in terms of cost effectiveness and all the demands in terms of increased responsibility.

The role of the SBM has changed dramatically over the past few years as more schools seek greater freedom from the Local Authority. Historically, it may not always have been necessary for a SBM to have any specific qualifications other than a good level of education and a range of experience.

That has changed and, today, the SBM will probably have a finance related qualification, or even be a qualified accountant. Over time a number of qualifications have been developed which recognise the qualities needed e.g. The Certificate of School Business Management (CSBM). This aims to provide participants with the skills and expertise to perform the role of school business manager and ultimately to improve school effectiveness. Many former post holders have undertaken these qualifications on a part time basis while the role is developing in their school.

In addition the SBM might have a banking, insurance or premises related background with a qualification and experience in the construction Industry or other relevant area.

Key elements of my role

A typical secondary school will employ over 200 staff with at least half of these being members of the support staff team. In my case, with two schools, there are over 130 teachers and 300 support staff. A major part of my role is managing this wide range of support staff and the variety of jobs they undertake, from a part-time member of the cleaning team to a full-time highly qualified specialist in finance or ICT. Staff recruitment and managing staff performance and absence are interesting facets of the role but can be time consuming.

Managing the Finance Team is obviously a very important part of the role. The size of the team will depend on the size of the school and how much is done 'in-house' in terms of functions like pay roll for example. However, it is not unusual for a large secondary school to have a fairly 'lean team' of 2 to 3 additional finance and personnel members of staff in addition to the SBM.

As the SBM in a two-school Multi Academy Trust I am on the leadership team for both schools and attend Academy Trust meetings. Apart from finance in both schools, I am responsible for the line-management and leadership of staff in Human Resources, premises, catering and the attached sports centre teams.

Five finance staff report directly to me. Three of these are employed to work across both schools, one focusing on the HR function, while two work only in one school to allow for separation of duties.

The premises manager works across both schools and is responsible for the site teams and cleaning teams on at each school, as well as overseeing all contractors.

We have a catering manager at each school who manages the kitchen staff and the sports centre manager is responsible for all sports assistants.

The ability to interact with a range of people is an important personal attribute. A typical day for me might start with a site meeting for a construction project where issues to do with the cavity wall are discussed, and end with a meeting of the Trustees where falling demographics for the next 3 years and the resulting impact on pupil numbers, and hence income, are a serious issue for discussion. This is the beauty of the role; no two days are ever the same. It is fast paced and varied and involves constant re-prioritising.

In order to be effective, the SBM must be fully conversant with what is going on in the organization, both on a day-to-day level and strategically. Thus, I believe that is crucial for the SBM to be a fully-fledged member of the Senior Leadership Team. This can involve participating in a lot of meetings, particularly if more than one school is involved but it is essential if you are to make fully informed decisions which underpin the strategic priorities for the school and to be an effective and valued member of the team.

How might a change of status impact on the role of the SBM?

New school responsibilities

Conversion to academy status can mean changes in role for an incumbent SBM. Yet the extent of the change in the role of SBM in an academy will depend on a number of factors. For example, if the school was not a cheque book holding school, and accustomed to buying in a lot of support from the Local Authority, then the SBM may feel anxious at losing that support.

New responsibilities will include the Academy Trust being the employer, the admission authority, and totally responsible for the premises and health and safety matters. It is noticeable that as academy conversion has gained traction Local Authorities are becoming more adept at operating in the market place of service provision which is also populated now by many commercial businesses. It is much more of a 'buyer's market' than in the early days of conversion.

Professional firms, for example those specialising in legal issues and accountancy, are becoming more expert in academy requirements and their services are also readily available if needed. I have found it very satisfying to source quotes from a commercial perspective and to buy in services from a wider range of providers which helps ensure value for money.

If the school was previously a foundation school and was already outsourcing many support services then the transition to academy status will be relatively painless.

Financial reporting

For almost all converter schools the one area that will require consideration is the additional financial reporting requirements that come as a result of being an exempt charity and a company limited by guarantee. Accounting procedures and requirements mirror commercial company accounting practice and are quite different from practice in the maintained school sector.

For an academy, the financial year follows the academic year, which can be an advantage in terms of supporting the curriculum. Year-end statutory accounts have to be prepared which comply with both Charity requirements and the Education Funding Agency (EFA) requirements, audited by a recognised firm of accountants, and filed at Companies House.

The EFA also requires various financial returns in addition to the statutory accounts and seeks reassurance that the academy finances are well controlled and managed in much more detail than the Local Authority did previously. As an example, it requires the Accounting Officer, (which is always the Headteacher) to sign and submit a Value for Money Statement at the financial year-end.

Although there is a range of guidance available, it is my experience that preparation of the year- end accounts can be daunting and very time consuming for the new academy SBM if they do not have some accountancy experience. In this situation schools may buy in the services of an accountant to oversee the year-end account preparation or, if the audit firm is large enough, the academy may be able to use the services of someone uninvolved in the actual audit process for the school.

Effective money management

Cash management is another key area that will require careful monitoring and forecasting:

running out of cash is clearly not an option! I have found the opportunity to manage cash using on-line banking is an advantage and offers real control in this respect. For example, we have offered parents the opportunity to buy laptops and the facility for them to pay in regular installments by direct debit is very easy to manage and monitor.

An academy has the freedom to invest surplus funds according to the policy laid down by its trustees, and could include, for example, investing in fixed rate bonds for longer periods of time in order to maximize returns.

Capital funding

An academy is able to bid directly to the Education Funding Agency for capital funding. This facility is available annually, is operated on a bid process where the criteria for priorities are set by the Education Funding Agency. Newly converted academies have the opportunity to bid for funds almost immediately and the SBM will probably be central to preparing the bids needing to pull together the various elements; timescale, funding required, evidence of need etc. I have found that to be successful in this process is very rewarding, both personally for the School Business Manager and for the academy. I felt a huge sense of achievement when we were able finally to see the back of 40 year old temporary classrooms after continually failing to persuade the Local Authority to address this issue!

Job satisfaction

I really enjoy my job and would not want to go back to the more restrictive days of Local Authority control. If you, as the SBM, are willing to embrace the additional freedoms academy status can bring then I am sure you too will find the role very fulfilling. The additional EFA reporting requirements can, on occasion, be frustrating but must be considered in the context of academies being funded from the public purse and the need for greater accountability that this brings. For me academy status is definitely the way forward and, if you are about to support your school down this route, I hope this guide will give you some comfort and confidence.

1c. Case Study – The Primary Experience

Jayne Harrison, School Business Manager of Violet Way Academy, describes her pivotal role in the academy conversion of the school and explains how this has developed in the new structure.

My role in conversion

I was asked to take the lead in planning and managing the conversion of the school to academy status. Having an understanding of the theory of change through my degree work, this was an exciting opportunity for me to put some of it into practice.

The key skills needed include the ability to think creatively; to plan, drive and support the change; to work effectively with external agencies such as unions; to communicate successfully with parents, the community and a range of other stakeholders.

An important objective in any discussion was to achieve a 'win/win' solution. According to Covey:

> *"Win/win means that agreements or solutions are mutually beneficial, mutually satisfying. With a win/win solution all parties feel good about the decision and feel committed to the action plan".* (1999: page 203)

The School Business Managers' Competency Framework (SBMCF – The National College of Teaching and Leadership) is another useful resource for all aspects of the SBM's role as it identifies the different levels at which a SBM might operate in different structures. In particular in Section 3 there is a helpful summary of the skills the SBM will need in facilitating change and I summarise some of it below:

The SBM is able to:

- Plan, lead and implement change in and across wider areas of school development
- Understand and use effective planning techniques
- Understand stakeholder expectations and how they influence the process
- Articulate the benefits of innovation to the school, its customers and other stakeholders
- Lead proportionate innovation in their own areas of responsibility
- Organise the resources, time and support required for innovation
- Evaluate proposals and plans for the practical implementation of ideas and approve those that appear viable
- Communicate regularly with parties affected by change
- Understand how to manage and support people through organisational change

My role post conversion

Overview of my current role

As a SBM the main areas for which I am responsible are:

- Finances
- Human resources

- Health and safety
- Premises
- Management of support services including extended schools and communications

Working within the primary sector my responsibilities can vary from operational to strategic across all these areas of responsibility. It is important to me that my expertise in the role and my focus on the business side of the academy enables the Principal to focus on teaching and learning, ensuring standards are maintained as an outstanding provider.

My role as a member of the Senior Leadership Team (SLT) is understood and respected within the school community, including governors. Our academy support staff structure is included at the end of this chapter. In addition, I have financial responsibility for the on-site nursery and care club budgets and directly manage 8 members of staff in our Care Club that operates from 7.00 am – 8.45 am and 2.45 pm – 6.15 pm, for 50 weeks of the year.

Strategic role

An important strategic focus for the SLT is to ensure that both the academy as an institution, and our children, are equipped to meet the complex demands of the 21st century.

Gerver has described the school of the future as being:

> "...about understanding the learning and management of that learning; it is about creating flexible, almost liquid environments that can change and develop as quickly as the world around them." (2010: page 74)

For me this means contributing to school improvement planning. For example ICT has recently been a particular focus for us and it is my operational responsibility to make sure we comply with the best value principles of challenge, compare, compete and consult when purchasing resources. Then I have a strategic responsibility to look ahead and try to 'future proof' the system.

A new ICT curriculum infrastructure is about to be installed in the school which will mean the academy is ready to meet the needs of touch technology and connectivity but still has some capacity to cope with developments we are not yet aware of.

Financial role

Since achieving academy status in June 2011, my responsibility for finance has become more strategic. Whist managing a budget as a community school required effective maintenance and monitoring, cash flow was never a consideration. If we spent more one month then it didn't matter, as the budget was annual. As an academy cash flow is critical as monies are paid into the bank on a monthly basis. This required a rethink of how we spent money.

It was an important part of my strategic role to develop short term operational and longer term strategic plans, meaning that larger items are 'saved' whilst protecting the monthly commitments. This is clearly expected by the EFA as the Academies Financial Handbook 2013:14 states:

> 'The academy trust must prepare financial plans so as to secure its short term and long-term financial health'.

Again the SBMCF in Section 5 refers to the different levels relating to managing resources and the skills required by the SBM are clearly identified and summarised below:

The SBM is able to:

- Manage budgets and maintain accurate financial information to assist effective monitoring to achieve the school's educational goals and priorities
- Maximise income through lettings and extended services provision
- Provide and present accurate accounts of the school performance
- Undertake effective procurement processes to ensure value for money
- Benchmark information against other similar schools with a view to maximising school efficiencies
- Give accurate accounts of the school performance

Other elements of my role

Responsibility for HR and, in particular, managing varied and sometimes complex teams requires me to have a very different set of skills to those required for finance. As part of my professional development I had the opportunity to learn about understanding teams, managing self and others and communication.

Firstly, I had to learn about myself. Goleman states that:

> 'From self-awareness – understanding one's emotions and being clear about one's purpose – flows self-management, the focused drive that all leaders need to achieve their goals'. (2002:45)

Developing productive relationships with colleagues allows me to build, lead and develop successful teams. The SBMCF (Section 4) highlights the different skills and levels at which SBMs many find themselves working. Sometimes I will be working at an operational level, for example, monitoring quality of work. But I also work at the strategic level: I am currently planning how we will implement free school meals for all children aged 4 – 7 which includes working with multiple teams and external agencies on a capital project to extend the kitchen requiring me to focus on timescales, priorities and sustainability.

A key document for academies

The Academies Financial Handbook (The Handbook) sets out the duties and responsibilities of academy trusts which have a funding agreement with the Secretary of State for Education (1.1.1). This document makes clear the responsibilities of the trust's Accounting Officer; in a single school this will be the Principal, in a Multi-Academy Trust structure the role will be undertaken by the Chief Executive or the Executive Principal. *See chapter 3 of the HM Treasury's Managing Public Money for a detailed guide.*

The Handbook also requires the Board to appoint finance staff that are suitably qualified or experienced to manage the financial systems according to the requirements of the EFA. A key role is described as the designated 'Principal Finance Officer' (2.1.7 Handbook) who is almost always the School Business Manager.

Section 2.1 of the Handbook clearly defines the expectations and responsibilities of the

'Principal Finance Officer' role and also recognises:

> *'many PFOs combine their specific financial responsibilities with a range of other support and leadership responsibilities in which the existence of a formal accountancy qualification may be less relevant.'*

This recognition is particularly welcome within the primary sector. Whilst managing a budget with rigour and robustness, the requirements of the role within this sector are often wide-ranging and typically not confined to finance.

Personal reflection

The autonomy that being an academy has brought still drives me and the reward is seeing the children's faces when they spend time on our art room, or have spent the afternoon on the woodland and come back covered in mud.

Yes – it can be scary; yes – it is challenging; but there is always someone to turn to: solicitors, accountants, other local academies, organisations like FASNA and NASBM and Primary Academy Associates to name but a few.

Having had the privilege of supporting the training of SBMs for a number of years, both within the primary and secondary sector, it is clear that many of the competencies required for school business management are a matter of confidence and opportunity. So often participants would comment 'I can't do that' when looking at the School Business Managers' Competency Framework, particularly as they looked to Advanced School Business Management (ASBM) and Extended School Business Management (ESBM) levels, but in reality, given the right support and knowledge many SBMs, especially in the primary sector, surprised themselves and found that they could.

References:

Covey, S (1999). *The 7 Habits of Highly Effective People.* Simon and Schuster

Gerver, R (2010). *Creating Tomorrow's Schools Today.* Continuum

Goleman, D. Boyatziz, R. McKee, A (2002). *The New Leaders.* Little Brown

The Academies Financial Handbook 2013. EFA

1d. Top Tips for School Business Managers and Governors

School Business Managers

1. The School Business Manager must have a clear job description outlining:
   - Key areas of responsibility with major elements identified
   - Within each area have defined lines of accountability:
     - accountable for whom
     - and accountable to whom
2. There should be a clear timeline of the key decisions and actions for each area of responsibility. For example:
   - A calendar of key finance events including budget setting, reports to governors, returns to the EFA etc
   - A Gantt chart or similar for any premises work being undertaken
   - An overview of HR responsibilities and when actions occur – performance management for example
3. The SBM should have focussed performance targets and a timeline for review so that they know how they are doing!
4. There should also be access to appropriate CPD as required
5. Look out for information on SBM accreditation by going to: www.gov.uk/government/ news/changes-to-nctls-school-business-management-programmes
6. There should be a Financial Procedures Manual outlining all the systems, processes, delegated powers, authorisation limits and other responsibilities for the management of the school finances

And for governors

1. Refer to Section 3.4 of our Effective Governance guide for more information about the financial responsibility of governors and the link with the Ofsted framework
2. Refer to Section 6.5 of our Effective Governance guide for more information about financial responsibility of governors when considering or converting to academy status
3. Ensure that you know the job description of the School Business Manager and how they relate to other members of staff
4. Be aware of the skills required, and the skills possessed, by the School Business Manager
5. Check the schools Financial Procedures Manual to ensure that it covers all that is required and that processes are followed
6. Ensure that the Headteacher reports on the Performance Management of the School Business Manager

Chapter 2

The role of governors

2a. Introduction

This chapter looks at the accountability role of governors and how to undertake the role effectively.

> **Focus of the chapter**
>
> This chapter focuses on the financial accountability role of governors and how this is linked to the work of the School Business Manager.
>
> **Key questions**
>
> - What are the key decisions which governors take with regard to ensuring financial probity? This may include:
>   - The employment of well qualified staff
>   - An appropriate and effective finance office structure
>   - Clear job descriptions for finance staff which ensure appropriate checks and balances
>   - Adherence to the Financial Procedures Manual etc
> - Are the responsibilities of the Finance Committee clearly spelt out and minuted?
> - How has the governing body ensured that there are governors with appropriate financial skills on the Finance Committee?
> - How do governors undertake their role in budget planning and monitoring?
> - Is the annual financial cycle reflected in the Governors' meeting calendar?
> - How do the Chair of the Finance Committee and the School Business Manager work together?
> - How do governors evidence that they scrutinise and challenge the financial management of the school?
> - Are the arrangements for audit clearly set out (also see Chapter 4)
> - Is there a Responsible Officer and is their role clearly understood?

Overview

The governing body should clearly identify the committee which will have responsibility for budget planning and monitoring. This may be a Resources Committee which also includes personnel and premises matters, or it may be a Finance Committee focused solely on the budget cycle and financial matters. The Terms of Reference should clearly set out what the responsibilities of governors are and include a meeting timetable for regular budget monitoring information. If a combined Resources Committee is used it is good practice to identify a 'Finance Lead' from within the committee if the Chair of Resources does not have appropriate financial skills.

Strategically the role of the governors is to ensure best value and that the school priorities are reflected in the budget allocations. For example, if a school priority identifies the need to employ a Family Liaison Worker, the budget discussions should make reference to this priority and identify the budget heading under which the cost will be noted. This process then clearly links the School Improvement Plan with budget expenditure. It may be appropriate for some or all of the anticipated cost in this example to be allocated to Pupil Premium funding.

The monitoring role of governors is to ensure the school can evidence the impact of this specific allocation. It is good practice for the Finance Committee to identify the potential costs of any school priority which may be spread over more than one financial year.

There are some specific requirements with regard to academies. A Responsible Officer (RO) should be appointed to undertake internal controls sampling on a termly basis. This person may be a governor, although not one on the Finance Committee, or a suitably qualified volunteer from the community. Some academies have a reciprocal arrangement whereby the SBM from one school acts as the RO. Whilst it may no longer be a requirement for smaller academies to maintain this role, it can be helpful to the SBM to have an extra pair of eyes ensuring accounting procedures are maintained.

A large academy with a budget of over £10 million or with capital assets of over £30 million must establish a separate Audit Committee. This committee should not be chaired by a member of the Finance Committee and has the responsibility of being the representatives of the governing body to whom the auditors' report. (*For details on Audit see Chapter 4 of this guide*).

Skills

It is important that at least some governors on the Finance Committee and Audit Committee have appropriate skills and qualifications. As well as the obvious accountant or financial qualifications, experience in insurance, contracting, managing a department budget, analytical skills and strategic budget planning are all useful skills.

Governing bodies need to have members who are able to analyse financial reports and have the personal strength and skills to ask challenging and probing questions.

It is important that the members of the Finance Committee or Resources Committee identify aspects of training which will help individual governors develop the required skills.

Relationship with the school

The SBM will usually be the main link between the Finance Committee and the school. The Chair of the Finance Committee and Chair of Audit Committee, if there is one, will need to work with the SBM and usually the Headteacher. The RO will need to liaise with the SBM to make monitoring visits and may also be invited to attend a Finance Committee if there are key issues arising from the RO's report.

Budget scrutiny and evidence of impact

An important function of the Finance Committee is to ensure that the school provides value for money. Activities such as benchmarking can be useful in providing comparisons and encourage the school to look at ways of reducing spending in an area, or help to highlight particular challenges for the school which may need to be reflected in strategic discussions.

An important area of scrutiny is the Pupil Premium Grant (PPG). The allocation of this money to strategies and activities must be monitored carefully and a process for evidencing impact identified. The important point is that the government will expect the PPG to enable the school to support the qualifying pupils so that they not only make progress but 'accelerated' progress, narrowing the gap between them and the progress of other pupils.

Ofsted

Obviously, it is important that governors are aware of how Ofsted may view their role with regard to the school's finances. To this end we have included a separate section on this in this chapter.

Similarly, Chapter 4 will look at audit and the role governors must play in the audit process. Chapter 5 will look at procurement and how governors must ensure that there are proper procedures in place and value for money is achieved. Chapter 6 on Premises and Facilities Management looks at the role of governors in health and safety pertaining to the physical aspects of the school. The statutory requirement for governors to ensure the safety and well-being of staff and pupils is also an important element of their role which is covered in our publication 'Effective Governance'.

2b. Governance and School Finances – What Ofsted are looking for

In this section we look at the Ofsted framework (2012) and what they expect a school to be doing with regard to finance.

In a well-governed school or academy the following features should be in place:

- Governors will be aware of the responsibilities of financial probity and have some knowledge of the relevant Financial Regulations documents including the relevant Financial Procedures Manual
- Some governors will have a deeper understanding of financial practices and requirements
- Some governors will have the ability to analyse financial reports and ask probing questions
- Appropriate training will be undertaken for relevant governors
- An appropriate committee structure with clear terms of reference and identification of delegated powers will be established
- There will be an appropriate reporting cycle to the full Governing Body from the Finance Committee

According to the Inspection Framework, when a school or academy is inspected the Inspectors should consider how well governors:

- Ensure solvency and probity and that the financial resources made available to the school are managed effectively
- Use the pupil premium and other resources to overcome barriers to learning, including reading, writing and mathematics

In what follows we will take a look at two elements which underpin this: **Financial Management** and **Budgeting**. We will consider how governors can demonstrate they carry out these functions effectively. Two other elements will be covered in later chapters: **Audit** (Chapter 4) and **Procurement and Contracts** – securing value for money (Chapter 5).

Financial management and the role of governors

The key questions governors need to ask to ensure they meet the Ofsted criteria for effective financial management are:

- How do governors ensure solvency and probity and that the financial resources of the school are managed effectively particularly with regard to procurement of goods and services?
- How do governors monitor the allocation and impact of the pupil premium?
- Have the relevant Financial Regulations been approved by the governing body?
- Are the provisions of the Financial Regulations appropriate to the needs of the school in terms of decision-making limits?
- Are there appropriate Terms of Reference for the Finance Committee with clear delegated powers including the responsibility to review and keep up to date all financial regulations and policies?
- Are the Financial Regulations reviewed on an annual basis?

- Do some governors have relevant financial experience or expertise?
- How will the governing body ensure that this is evidenced together with a succession plan for future?
- How will Finance Committee members and, to a lesser extent all governors, demonstrate that they have the ability to exert a robust approach to the monitoring and evaluation of school financial practices?

The above questions identify the core knowledge or overview which is appropriate for all governors.

The Schools Financial Value Standard (SFVS) was introduced in 2012 for maintained schools. This recognises the importance of establishing a formal audit process to ensure that public funds are safeguarded and that schools make decisions that deliver best value for the taxpayer, not necessarily the cheapest option but one which delivers the best result for the education of the pupils. Essentially the process should provide a framework for rational decisions that can be robustly defended if challenged by governors or external agencies.

www.gov.uk/government/publications/schools-financial-value-standard-and-assurance

The SFVS is not intended for schools outside of the control of local authorities. In the case of an academy, a separate Financial Regulations document exists with quite different reporting and account presentation requirements.

The detail and focus of financial matters will be considered most effectively by a committee which should be chaired by a governor with appropriate financial expertise and understanding. It is important that at least some members of the Finance Committee have experience in finance, budget management and control. An understanding of the requirements of separation of duties within the school finance office is also important.

Key areas to understand are identified below and are applicable to all schools. It is particularly important that governors in an academy understand how the financial responsibilities and reporting requirements differ from those for a LA maintained school.

The school budget

Generally, all governors should have a broad understanding of the school budget: its size, where it comes from and factors which may affect the budget. They should be able to answer the following questions:

- By which route does the school receive its budget – the EFA or LA?
- How is the budget determined?
- What are the fixed components of the budget?
- What are the variable components of the budget?
- What items of the budget, if any, are specific to the school?
- What was the outcome of the last external audit?
- What is the process for preparation of the draft budget for approval?

The detail of the school budget, and how it is to be allocated, will be the responsibility of a Finance or Resources Committee. However, the principles underpinning the budget should be agreed by the full governing body. For example, a change in curriculum provision could result in increased staffing needs with an impact on the budget.

The Finance Committee must be established with clear terms of reference, its delegated powers identified and agreed and minuted by the full governing body.

It should be clear how the Chair of the Finance Committee will work with the Headteacher, SBM and Senior Leadership Team to prepare the budget. It also needs to be clear how Chairs of other Committees have an input into budget planning.

The Finance Committee may feel that it is more appropriate to consider a draft budget and not be too involved in the earlier planning stages. Part of the budget discussion should identify that costings for key school priorities have been included in the draft.

It should be clear who is responsible for budget monitoring and day to day management within the school. The Finance Committee should have regular reports and have the delegated responsibility to determine any corrective action which needs to be taken to keep the budget on target. A clear meeting cycle, which enables effective reporting to the full governing body, should be established.

It is useful for the Finance Committee to seek benchmarking information to compare budget allocations and costs of services or insurances with other similar schools. This can be a useful exercise in identifying any budget area which is significantly higher or lower than similar schools. The committee should then identify the reasons for the variance and take any appropriate decisions.

The Pupil Premium is a new focus for Ofsted and governors should be able to identify how the additional money has been allocated, and what the impact is particularly in terms of reading, writing and mathematics. The Finance Committee should receive reports identifying the application of the pupil premium and the impact it has had. This would be reported to the full Governing Body.

Audit arrangements

Audit is covered in Chapter 4 in more detail. However, some of the key issues for governors facing an Ofsted Inspection will be:

- Are there appropriate internal controls arrangements? This function should monitor the implementation of the agreed Financial Regulations. The role may be undertaken by a governor or be included as part of the audit arrangements. Academies have to appoint a Responsible Officer
- What are the arrangements for an external audit? An external audit is not a statutory requirement for LA maintained schools and many do not do this especially if they are not a cheque book holding school

If the school does manage its own banking arrangements it is important to be able to demonstrate that an objective and transparent audit of the school's finances has been obtained. The principle should be agreed by the full governing body with the Finance Committee agreeing arrangements and charges. Internal controls may be organised from within the governing body but there needs to be a clear role description and reporting process.

- What are the arrangements for discussing the management letter as a result of the audit? The Finance Committee should be responsible for this and report findings and consequent actions to the full governing body

Procurement including Insurances and contracts

This is covered in more detail in Chapter 5. However, some of the key issues for governors facing an Ofsted Inspection will be:

- Does the school have procedures for the procurement of goods and services to ensure all legal requirements are met? This may be a more complex process for a new academy as the LA no longer has responsibility for the provision of some services. In addition to insurances, service areas to consider include payroll and pension, IT, property management, pupil support and legal support
- Do financial regulations adopted by the school identify arrangements for insurance policy and contract review arrangements and timescales? The Finance Committee should ensure that best practice is observed when approving insurance arrangements and contract charges and undertake regular benchmarking or comparison of charges

The key responsibilities of the Chair of Governors in relation to finance are to ensure that:

- A committee is established to focus on the key financial responsibilities reporting regularly to the full governing body meetings
- An appropriate and effective budget setting and monitoring process is established
- There is an effective audit process that delivers the necessary accountability

The inspection outcomes

Outstanding descriptors

Through highly effective, rigorous planning and controls, governors ensure financial stability, including the effective and efficient management of financial resources such as the pupil premium funding. This leads to the excellent deployment of staff and resources to the benefit of all groups of pupils.

Good descriptors

Governors ensure the efficient management of financial resources. This leads to the effective deployment of staff and resources.

2c. Case Study – The Primary Experience

Richard Barnard, Chair of Governors at Robinswood Primary Academy, Gloucester, describes how his Finance Committee undertakes the responsibility for financial probity.

Robinswood is a two-form entry primary academy in a suburb of Gloucester with a high level of social deprivation, where around half the pupils are in receipt of free school meals.

Key decisions for governors

It is now essential for all governing bodies, not just those planning to convert to academy status, to look very seriously at the way their school financial arrangements are managed. That the government considers this an important element of 'effective governance' is evidenced by their focus on the role of a SBM, the availability of grants in certain circumstances to support this function and the inclusion of the governors' responsibility for financial solvency and probity in the Ofsted framework.

One of the first things to do is to look at the staffing structure in your finance team and assess whether there is a need for the appointment of a more appropriately qualified lead person and ensure that there are clear job descriptions identifying separation of duties. If you need to make changes here you might be able to source additional funding, or you may be able to collaborate with other schools if appropriate. If there is a need for restructuring governors must ensure good HR practice. A budget for upgraded IT equipment for the finance team should also be identified as a necessary cost. All of this is good evidence of governors acting strategically.

Depending on your type of school there will be a different financial management handbook to follow. For academies this is the Academies Financial Handbook and for maintained schools there is often a Local Authority equivalent. It is the responsibility of governors to ensure adherence to the relevant manual. If you are considering conversion to academy status you need to ensure that the school finance personnel thoroughly understand the changes to financial practice and accounting procedures that this will entail.

Governors of an academy must also make two other decisions – to appoint external auditors and to appoint a Responsible Officer who will conduct internal controls checks, usually on a termly basis. Many community schools also have a similar appointment. When we appointed auditors we looked at three firms and were very keen to use one which could demonstrate knowledge of the educational sector. We also looked very carefully, with best value principles in mind, at what was included in the fee before making our decision.

Skills – Have we got the right people on the Finance Committee?

It is important that the Chair of the Finance Committee and other members of the committee have relevant skills. We have an independent accountant as our finance chair and other committee members bring experience of budget planning, budget management and monitoring or have a financial business background.

To evidence our skills all governors undertake a skills audit on an annual basis and we then confirm our membership of committees with reference to this audit. This ensures that we are using people to the best advantage and enables us to identify gaps in skills, or potential gaps due to planned resignations, and take appropriate actions to secure replacements. This is in keeping with the planned changes the DfE are making to the appointment of new governors.

We feel that it is important that as many governors as possible, and certainly those on the Finance Committee, should have regular training in monitoring the impact of finance decisions. This could be led by the SBM in terms of identifying the actual budget spend on a school priority, with the Headteacher presenting the school evaluation processes and success criteria. It would be the role of governors to verify that the evaluation was robust and that there was evidence of the success criteria. How, and to what effect, the school uses the pupil premium grant is a key area where this sort of process involving governor monitoring will help to evidence 'effective governance'.

Our Finance Committee is kept informed of all government initiatives, potential local demographic changes and any other factors which could affect our budget allocation. In this way we can be strategic in planning for future developments, making such adjustments as are necessary in a systematic way, and plan effectively for potential building projects.

The role of governors in financial planning and monitoring

Planning and monitoring needs to be done in a systematic way and we tend to follow the same cyclical pattern year on year. We have an on-going outline 3–5 year financial plan but two things drive our annual cycle. These are:

- Ensuring that more detailed financial plans for the year are in line with our strategic objectives linked clearly to school improvement
- Agreeing an annual schedule of meetings to monitor the budget and comply with the accounting process.

The Finance Committee monitors budget performance on a termly basis. This is the opportunity for governors to challenge the school on evidencing the impact on standards of particular allocations, pupil premium or any school specific strategy including, for example, the employment of an attendance officer.

We also find it informative to look at how the individual budget headings are performing against the approved budget allocation. Careful scrutiny here can sometimes flag up potential under or overspends which may need some corrective action. In terms of financial probity it is important that these issues are recorded as well as any subsequent actions. The reasons for both under and overspends need to be carefully identified and the potential impact on the end of financial year outcome recognised.

On an annual basis we look at benchmarking data to understand how we are performing in budget terms against similar schools. This can help to support school priorities. If we appear to be over spending in any area it enables us to identify the reasons and link this spend to our school circumstances and priorities.

Another important annual agenda item for us is the review of our pay policy (in tandem with our personnel committee) ensuring a strong link between pay and performance. This is especially important in light of the changes to pay progression from September 2013. We also have our own system of reward for teachers based on small 'treats', a voucher for a local meal out for example, which is well liked.

As part of the budget cycle and preparation of accounts we review our Best Value Statement, relevant contracts, banking arrangements and financial procedures especially authorisation limits to ensure they are still appropriate for our needs. As our school does not trigger the threshold for a separate audit committee, it is the finance committee which takes the lead here in meeting with the auditors to discuss the annual accounts, and to report and approve the accounts before they are presented to the full governing body.

Liaison with the School Business Manager

Our chair of finance meets with the School Business Manager on a monthly basis. This enables the chair to discuss a range of data and plan with the School Business Manager the most appropriate items for the finance committee agenda.

The chair of finance will interrogate the financial data in some detail including that relating to pupil premium, catering, free school meals, SEN and pupil mobility in order to have a good understanding of the financial health of the school and pick up any future trends which need further discussion.

These meetings help to establish an open and honest relationship between the School Business Manager, the Headteacher and the finance committee. If any urgent action needs to be taken the chair of finance is authorised to do so in consultation with the School Business Manager and Headteacher.

Evidence that governors scrutinise and challenge financial management of the school

The minutes of meetings need clearly to identify decisions about budget allocations which relate to the school's strategic vision and priorities. At the termly meetings governors should ask questions about the impact the money is having on standards and again the minutes need to record this carefully. In our case the Chair of Finance will also report on the monthly meetings with the School Business Manager which demonstrates good communication and that the committee agenda picks up any relevant matters raised at these meetings.

The procedures with regard to purchasing, procurement and contract renewal must comply with the Financial Procedures Manual. The termly report from the Responsible Officer should look at a sample of these transactions and also report that the agreed authorisation limits are being adhered to.

All governors should be kept informed about the discussions and actions taken by the finance committee through circulation of minutes and the chair reporting to the full governing body. We do not feel that this is an opportunity to revisit decisions but it is important that all governors understand the reasons for financial decisions and that there should be effective liaison with other committees which will evidence scrutiny and challenge. Staffing decisions will usually involve input from both finance and personnel committees.

Academies have to have an external audit and we see this as one of the best ways to evidence good financial management.

Recommendations for governors on the Finance Committee:

- Ensure the staffing structure is suitable and is well led. If appropriate, participate in the appointment of new staff especially a School Business Manager
- Ensure all finance staff and governor finance committee members have relevant, well focused professional development and keep up to date with changes to procedures and government policies which impact on budget allocations
- Ensure at least the chair of the committee has relevant financial experience and that other members are skilled at 'reading' balance sheets
- Be strategic – plan ahead, particularly in respect of potential changes to pupil numbers or local circumstances
- Establish good internal controls systems and appoint an effective Responsible Officer
- Appoint an auditor with experience in the educational sector
- Don't be afraid to ask for explanations or ask the 'idiot' question. Chances are that someone else has been hoping you would do just that

Primary schools sometimes find it difficult to appoint governors with the requisite skills particularly financial expertise. The School Business Manager from a local secondary school may be prepared to join your governing body. Or try making a personal approach to local businesses. However small these local businesses are, someone will have experience in strategic planning, budget preparation and monitoring which might transfer to the school setting. The local manager of a national chain store or supermarket can also bring useful expertise to a governing body.

2d. Case Study – The Secondary Experience

Brian Whitfield, Chair of the Nunthorpe Academy Trust, and Nigel Goodall, Director of Business and Finance from Nunthorpe Academy, Middlesbrough explain how governors undertake their role in ensuring financial probity

Nunthorpe Academy is an 11-19 mixed, all ability comprehensive, which converted to academy status in 2011. It has approximately 1500 students. There are 200 staff (full time equivalent) and an annual income of about £7.2m. The school has managed to date, to have an operating surplus of approximately £100,000.

Additionally, the school manages a successful adult learning business, which turns over in excess of £110k annually.

Introduction

The school and governing body has always been passionate about financial probity, efficiency and accountability, believing that being 'masters of our own destiny' in financial terms ensures ongoing success for the students, parents and staff.

As a governing body, we are clear about the importance of setting strategic priorities but delegate day to day financial decisions to the Principal and senior team. These decisions must be taken in the context of the appropriate Strategic and Improvement Plans, which are monitored by governors.

How do governors undertake their role in budget planning and monitoring?

General principles

One of the first things governors did to secure improvement in financial accountability was to recruit a Director of Business and Finance (DBF) with a corporate financial background in banking. This appointment has enabled the school to be confident in financial planning and reap the benefits of astute financial management.

The full governing body is involved in producing a Strategic Plan for the school. We now do this on a rolling five-year basis to enable a broad financial overview to be identified at this stage to ensure on-going financial sustainability, viability and improvement of our academy.

A more detailed three-year rolling strategic budget plan is drawn up to ensure that we achieve as smooth a transition as possible year on year. Therefore, the Board (Governing Body) receives budget recommendations in the context of a three-year financial plan and a five-year strategic plan.

In terms of raising standards and school improvement, the overarching Strategic Plan is 'fleshed out' on an annual basis to determine the more detailed and operational Nunthorpe Improvement Plan.

Governing Body Committee structure

To facilitate the focus on financial management the Board (Governing Body) has established a Resources Development Committee (RDC) which meets each half term with additional meetings for extraordinary needs, such as a capital project for example.

The RDC is chaired by the Chairman of the Board and enjoys fully delegated autonomy to run the business of the school providing half termly reports to the Full Board.

In brief, the Resources Development Committee:

1. Approves the annual budget for the academy (before it is presented for ultimate approval at the Full Board (in line with academies legislation)
2. Monitors the budget each half term through half termly monitoring reports from the DBF
3. Monitors the academy cash flow position each half term through cash flow reports produced by the DBF
4. Receives twice yearly monitoring reports from the Responsible Officer (RO) (one of our governors who is financially competent but not a member of this committee)
5. Receives an annual audit report from the academy's accountants – the audit is completed annually, but we stay in regular contact with auditors in terms of practical advice, legislative changes and our attendance at their academy information forums three times a year
6. Ensures that the Directors' declaration of business interests register is kept up to date

Strategic priorities

At least one of our strategic priorities each year has a specific financial focus.

In the year 2012–2013 one priority focused on securing an 'Outstanding' Ofsted judgment which we achieved in April 2013.

The financial element of this priority was based on ensuring that key staffing changes and new appointments could be accommodated within the budget.

A previous strategic priority focused on taking over the failing adult education service run by the Local Authority and located in our school, with the intention of turning it into a success and an income generating opportunity.

This entailed making a budget allocation for an appointment of Extended School Director- with an 'entrepreneurial edge' - who understood both the provision of high quality community learning (where many of our 'day' staff now work as course tutors also) and the magical art of effective, profitable lettings management!

We set up a separate business to run the adult learning as part of our commitment to community activities and we now have a £110k+ annual turnover with an operating surplus of about £10k, 99-100% customer satisfaction surveys; and an annually updated course offer which responds directly to customer demand. There were fewer than 300 learners in 2006 but we now have 1100 adult learners at any one time. This success has more than justified the original budget allocation for the Extended School Director.

How do our governors ensure robust financial accountability at all levels of the academy?

This is done through our Financial Management and Procedures Handbook, which is reviewed and approved each year by the Resources and Development Committee.

The Handbook is absolutely clear in its insistence on robust procedures and financial accountability. The following extracts illustrate this:

1. All orders have to be signed off (at request stage) by both the account holder(s) and their line manager
2. Purchases with single items/value in excess of £500 need to be countersigned by a member of the Senior Leadership Team
3. Purchases with a value in excess of £5000 must also be countersigned by the Principal
4. Invoices with a value of more than £25k need to be authorised by the Principal and Chair of the Academy Trust prior to payment
5. Budget overspends (subject to satisfaction within overall Academy financial performance) can only be authorised by the Principal and the Director of Business and Finance jointly.
6. The Responsible Officer scrutinises all such procedures on a random sample basis – minimum twice a year, with a maximum of 3 times a year
7. We have an annual audit from our accountants – again where scrutiny is applied

In conclusion

We are proud of the clarity of our financial management vision and strategy at Nunthorpe. Through resolute commitment to that vision and strategy in all the financial decisions made by the academy we continue to witness our academy's rapid improvements – securing better life chances for our students every day through those improvements.

Brian Whitfield
Chairman of the Nunthorpe Academy Trust

Nigel Goodall
Director of Business and Finance

2e. Top Tips for Governors on the Finance Committee

1. Refer to Section 3.4 of our Effective Governance guide to ensure all governors are aware of their strategic financial responsibility and the link with the Ofsted framework
2. Ensure that you have a completed skills audit for all governors identifying appropriate financial skills for members of the Finance or Resources Committee
3. Ensure that there are clear terms of reference for the Finance Committee or that they are included in the remit of a Resources Committee
4. Ensure that the limit of the delegated powers of the committee are identified and minuted
5. Ensure that spending and, if you are an academy, cash flow, are monitored regularly and reported to the Finance Committee
6. Ensure that meetings focus on budget monitoring linked to school priorities and that evidence of impact can be demonstrated
7. Ensure that minutes of meetings identify how the Governors challenge the finances through questions and appropriate follow up
8. Ensure that all governors are aware of the relevant Financial Procedures Manual (for academies this is the Financial Handbook issued by the Education Funding Agency) and that they are aware of the delegated funding limits within the document
9. Ensure that the Financial Procedures Handbook is reviewed annually – if only to remind governors of its contents
10. Ensure that there is an appropriate reporting process to the full governing body on at least a termly basis
11. Undertake appropriate professional development
12. Ensure that timings of governors' meetings allows for the approval and submission of financial information by the required dates. See the DFE yearly planner

Chapter 3

School Business Planning

3a. Introduction

This chapter looks at the role of the School Business Manager in strategic business planning as a member of the Senior Leadership Team.

Focus of the chapter

This chapter will give examples of how School Business Managers contribute to the strategic planning of the school and the school development plan.

The key questions a SBM should think about, and governors should ask, are:

- Does the School Development Plan (SDP) include identification of what is needed to support curriculum provision and pupil progress such as an IT upgrade?
- Is such a need related to a school priority and a potential cost identified?
- How are governors involved in the decision making process?
- How is the SBM involved in the determination of school priorities and the SDP?
- Are high cost projects spread over a number of years?
- Is there a short and medium term business plan identifying potential risks to budget projections?
- Do you regularly consider the potential impact on your school of local and national decisions and initiatives?
- How far ahead do you project a business plan taking into consideration predictions of admission numbers, known expenditure, planned maintenance, forecast income etc, and how do you make the Senior Leadership Team and governors aware of any concerns as a result of this forward projection?
- How effective is your business planning in terms of supporting pupil progress?

Context

From a purely financial viewpoint the school is a business; the largest schools may have a budget of £10 million and a workforce of 350 or more. Even very small community schools still under the auspices of the Local Authority have a responsibility to function as a 'going concern' in business terms.

It has become increasingly clear that schools need professional business support which goes beyond school finance and into many other disciplines, from HR through to site maintenance and project management, with a raft of skills in-between. Individuals with these skills are being sought by schools and governing bodies, in order to help determine and deliver their vision.

In 2009 the School Business Management Competency Framework (SBMCF) was introduced to support the growth and the ongoing development of school business managers. The competency framework provides a good basis for managers to develop the skill set they need to work in their school environment, some of which are included in the introduction to Chapter 1. The SBMCF is further supported by a full range of qualifications for SBMs. This is a reflection of the fact that SBMs are increasingly fulfilling critical roles in complex situations, managing large non-teaching workforces and being responsible for budgets and projects of considerable size. *Again, some of the relevant qualifications are identified in the introduction to Chapter 1.*

Overview

If a school has converted to an academy then the Funding Agreement makes reference to the academy following the Academies Financial Handbook. The Handbook makes the point that the Principal Finance Officer should have a leadership as well as a technical role within the academy. This is recommended because unless the SBM (who is the Principal Finance Officer) is a member of the Senior Leadership Team, and works closely with governors, they cannot provide the guidance and support required for strategic planning.

In June 2013 the DfE published its Review of Efficiency in the School System. This recognised that there was strong evidence supporting the appointment of a skilled Business Manager to play a prominent role in schools. This was often already the case in large secondary schools, but was less evident in small primary schools.

The importance of the SBM is further highlighted by the fact that in 2014 the DfE introduced a grant applicable to a group of three or more primary schools to support the employment of a SBM. At the time of going to press this grant was £25,000 and it was not conditional on conversion to academy status. Of course, the onus is on the schools to support the continued employment of the SBM.

In order for the above scenario of a shared SBM to be most effective, it will be important for the schools to have a shared vision and the commitment to allocating funding to finance the role. The opportunities for savings through collective purchasing or insurance contracts should more than compensate.

The role of SBM is more than just ensuring that the budget is balanced and monitored appropriately throughout the year. For example, it has developed to include being able to identify potential risks in relation to achieving strategic objectives and to make effective contingency plans, to identify improvements to school services and support the practical implementation of innovative ideas.

Strategic Planning is becoming ever more important as funding gets tighter. There is the need to plan further ahead than just the next year. This is more important as transitional arrangements end, the minimum funding guarantee is less protective and there are changes to funding formulas.

Obviously, the future is uncertain but some things can be foreseen. Demographic changes must be catered for; the need to bid for capital funding considered; the known changes to staff costs built in and planned for; planned developments costed. If schools are drawing up school improvement plans for several years ahead, it makes sense that similar financial planning parallels this. Governors and senior leadership may have great ambitions for the future but if the finances do not support those plans then they are worthless. Clearly, strategic planning will be meaningless unless the financial advice given is robust and accurate.

Summary

It is very clear that the SBM plays a pivotal role in forward strategic planning. The SBM needs to understand the school's priorities and be able to support or resist ideas based on the school's finances.

Our case studies describe the developing role of the SBM and the importance of strategic planning and contributing as part of the School Leadership Team.

3b. Case Study – The Primary Experience

Vikki England, School Business Manager of Glebe Academy, a newly converted primary academy with 230 pupils in Stoke-on-Trent, explains how she participates in strategic planning.

Strategic planning and monitoring process

My Executive Head recognises the important strategic role a School Business Manager (SBM) plays within a school and involves me alongside other members of the Senior Leadership Team (SLT) in the process of producing the School Development Plan (SDP). Subject leaders and governors also participate in the process and this, in turn, supports and strengthens the development of our whole school leadership capacity; an important consideration for a stand-alone converter such as ours. By this means we are gaining confidence to secure and use the academy freedoms to best effect for our school.

Our SDP leads to the Self-Evaluation Form (SEF) both of which are monitored on a half termly basis by the SLT. As SBM and a member of the SLT, I am involved in the evaluation process, taking an active part in the review and monitoring meetings. We analyse, scrutinise and dissect the data, both current and historic, to evaluate how well the school is performing against the priorities identified in the SDP. This meeting also gives us an opportunity to discuss any changes to legislation or new government initiatives or targets that may have a direct impact, either positive or negative, on our future plans.

The SDP is a continuous working document within school. To assist school leaders and governors immediate/accomplished priorities are highlighted in green, ongoing medium term priorities in yellow and longer-term priorities in red. Priorities move through the colour scheme until they are completed and drop off the plan when achieved or no longer needed.

Advantages of involving the SBM in strategic planning

I feel that my inclusion and participation at a high level in this wider strategic overview enables me to be more effective in undertaking my SBM responsibilities.

I am able at an early stage in the planning to identify and evidence the impact of allocating funding to longer term strategic priorities as well as having the ability to make informed operational decisions to improve the environment or cash flow as well as sometimes mitigating the effects of unplanned issues.

Working alongside my Executive Head and other senior leaders on longer term planning it is vital that I have a whole school overview of school priorities in order to assign, monitor and measure impact of financial investments across a range of areas.

As a very recent primary convertor academy, this year I am eager to oversee the huge benefits of being able to start measuring budget allocations against SDP priorities with a unified financial and academic year. I am sure this will support greater accuracy in evaluating the impact on improved pupil attainment and will focus the attention of governors and school staff on their accountability. This will also feed into considerations about performance at staff level to evidence a robust link to pay decisions and at governor level to evidence their ability to challenge and support as required by the Ofsted framework.

My contribution to the educational elements of the School Development Plan

In order to do this effectively I believe it is necessary to have a full understanding of school data and national statistics combined with a deep personal interest in keeping your knowledge up to date about changes in legislation and local or national education priorities. Understanding why the school is responding to these in a certain way is a vital element of being able to contribute to the educational discussions of the SDP and therefore being able to suggest appropriate budget allocations or changes.

This is as important a factor in the strategic development of the school as the need for the SBM to understand funding formulae and processes. Knowing how and why school priorities are identified, monitored and evaluated ensures that we plan a budget which will use available resources to support the decisions and increase our capacity to develop further.

I have specific responsibility for monitoring and evaluating Pupil Premium progress, reporting back to governors half-termly. This is directly referenced in the School Evaluation Form, RAISEonline evaluation and the School Development Plan. RAISEonline is a secure web-based system available to governors, schools and local authorities. Ofsted inspectors also use it to inform their inspections. Working in a highly deprived area means that this funding stream is a considerable income for the school and clearly has impact across several areas of the SDP. For two consecutive years our school has been recognised within the top 250 schools nationally for the achievement and progress made by this group of children.

Every change or initiative that I assist in developing and implementing within the SDP is put into place for the direct benefit of raising attainment and outcomes for pupils. This may be directly through the purchase of new educational equipment or indirectly through the strategic implementation of new HR policies, staffing structures, changing external service providers or pursuing capital investments.

As SBM my performance management targets, alongside other members of the SLT, are set and measured against the same criteria and rightly linked to evidenced educational outcomes. These reflect the criteria for the national standards for head teachers.

Involvement of governors

Since converting to an academy the Governing Body (GB) has been encouraged to develop smaller working groups with the Chair of each group recruited for their skills in a specific field i.e. finance, HR or community engagement. The Chairs from each group form the Core Group which meets on a monthly basis to receive and review income and expenditure reports, pupil progress information and is the key strategic group.

This group then reports back termly to the remainder of the GB, which retains its overall accountability and authority. Often, delegated power is given to the Core Group or other relevant sub-committee by the full GB, to ensure in-depth knowledge is applied and adherence to critical time frames.

The full GB is always consulted at the start of a significant project. I find that working with a smaller yet better informed group of governors as a specialist sub-committee means that an immense amount of skilled knowledge and scrutiny is applied to big financial projects, particularly if these are planned to stretch over several years. The small group with delegated responsibility is beneficial as decisions can be taken, a project approved and completed more quickly so that pupils are faster able to reap the rewards.

Forward planning

The nature of specific projects and factors such as scale, urgency, intended outcomes and financial investment required will predetermine how far ahead planning can reasonably take place. As SBM, I work closely with the SLT and relevant sub-committees to present a number of potential scenarios detailing advantages and disadvantages, timescales and projected costs for specific long-term projects. This helps us identify quickly the less favourable options and to agree which should be further investigated.

Most large-scale projects with my school are planned and agreed within a twelve month period and typically stretch across a maximum of three years. Planning beyond this period of time may be beneficial to some schools, however circumstances and government priorities change rapidly in the current educational climate and I feel that committing resources to projects beyond this period has the potential to restrict our school's future ability to respond to change. That said, projecting beyond the three-year period is part of our continuing development of the vision for the school and helps us to ensure committed projects have a relevance to potential future developments.

Budget cycle 'pinch points'

Having recently converted to an academy, the budget planning cycle this year will be far more streamlined sitting hand-in-hand with the production of the SEF and SDP.

During the summer term the budget and SEF will be developed as a combined process with the SDP in place from the very start of the new academic year. This undoubtedly will be reviewed with the release of the RAISEonline in the autumn. We work hard by continuing scrutiny of data to ensure that this will not present us with any surprises.

The alignment of the financial year with the academic year will, I hope, remove some of the budget 'pinch points'. Moving from a centralised Local Authority finance system is a monumental change for any school, SBM and finance team (regardless of academy status) and will go for the most part unnoticed by the rest of the school community.

The transition to academy status was certainly a 'pinch point' involving setting up our own systems and bank accounts and a significant learning curve. Maintaining sufficient cash flow has also been a significant challenge for me in the early stages of academy conversion.

Pinch points may occur at times of the year when teaching staff have pay rises backdated to the previous September and support staff have pay rises effective from April. It is important at these times that sufficient cash flow is maintained and ensuring that governors and SLT understand the need to manage resources appropriately is part of my reporting role to the governing body.

Another potential 'pinch point' is during the autumn term when the previous year's accounts have to be finalised, audited and lodged with the appropriate bodies before the end of December. Managing the additional meetings this requires with governors needs careful planning and is often subject to the availability of the auditors.

And finally...

The degree of trust placed in me by my Headteacher has brought greater fulfilment to my role but the challenges are clearly greater; my level of accountability is high and the need to deliver in the drive for excellence is extremely clear. The strategic overview I hold, linking the educational and financial priorities of the school is invaluable in assisting governors to have a greater awareness of the potential benefits of the future development. My role within SLT focusing on the implementation of a financial strategy based on 'best value' enables the teachers to focus more effectively on the educational and pupil related outcomes.

3c. Case Study – The Primary Experience in a Multi Academy Trust

Gill Baggley, School Business Manager, Chetwynd Primary Academy, Nottingham

As a Converter Academy, the basic principles of School Business Planning are no different to those followed as a Local Authority school. The changes come in the detail of the planning and the accountability in reporting.

I work closely with the Principal to cost the elements of the School Development Plan (SDP) which have a financial implication. Together we assess the faculty needs and involve our subject leaders in costing their preferred resources. We build this into our Budget Plan.

Examples of key issues we consider are: any known changes within staffing, subject priority developments, building and premises changes or improvements, all of which may affect our expenditure for the year. The educational elements of the SDP are generally constructed by the Principal and senior staff, however, I have an input to ensure the overall picture is sustainable.

Once we have the financial implications of all of the elements of the SDP, we present this to our governors for their approval. If there are elements of the plan which cause short-term cash shortages or even deficits, such as building projects, we need to make a case for a long-term benefit so governors can justify approval of reserves, to fund the short-term situation.

During the annual cycle priorities may change and there is the need to provide best value in all areas of expenditure, hence I am always monitoring our budget, looking for variances to budget and reasons for this. Key times are end of terms for resignations and the impact that may have, and holidays when larger building work projects may be in danger of overrunning the allocated budget.

It is my role to check our service providers, ensuring that they deliver their promised provision and look for financial savings, without compromising the outcomes.

For us, pupil numbers remain fairly stable and therefore we are able to predict our future budgets in line with current funding arrangements. The live birth rate in our area is increasing and our future problem is not having enough places for children who live within our catchment area. It is my responsibility to look at trends in pupil numbers and predict our likely expenditure for the next three to five years, in line with increasing staffing costs and inflation. The software we now use for developing budgets automatically allows for grade increments and can add inflation factors. We prefer to budget without inflation, either for costs or incomes, so all projections are on a 'comparable time value of money' basis. This is, of course, far more important when inflation is at higher levels, but we just find it easier to compare without having to consider the differing effects of inflation, looking always at the 'current cost' of goods and services.

There are many grants available to schools, some of them are direct from government, others are from other sources, each with different application processes.

As SBM, I am involved in ensuring that all government grants are spent in accordance with the Grant Conditions from the DfE and that the Principal is aware of the implications of these. Pupil Premium and PE/Sports Grants are just two examples of areas where Ofsted may check to ensure our provision meets the statutory requirements and that the educational outcomes for the children are measured and challenged.

In terms of applying for other grants, we work as a team with the Trust finance team to complete and then monitor successful bids.

On a monthly basis, I meet with the Principal, to discuss our cash flow and profiled expenditure for the closing period. This ensures that the Principal is fully briefed on the current financial position at all times.

Involved in this process is a detailed analysis of staff salaries for the particular month, ensuring that they have been paid in line with their current salary pay point as agreed by the Governing Body. Any additional payments or deductions need to be checked against reports submitted to the payroll provider.

In turn, this information is checked by the appointed auditors, who work for our Multi Academy Trust, checking the group accounts for the whole Trust.

As a Primary Academy, my colleagues in other schools will be able to identify with the varied challenges of working in a setting where the demands on your time go beyond those experienced by our colleagues in the secondary sector. We don't have private offices where we can shut the door and focus solely on 'numbers' all day. We are constantly distracted by the needs of young children, and the staff who rely on us, for just about everything. There is no hiding place...

I am also part of the Core Strategy Team for our school, constantly working to support our new Principal in the constant flux of an operational establishment.

I find myself relying on the Trust team to support me on technical accountancy matters when qualified people are on hand to give advice. This also is a training and confidence building relationship for me.

Primary school budgets, in my experience, do not, yet, allow for employing full time accountants or qualified HR staff. If asked, I would counsel any SBM who belongs to a school where the management are advocating conversion to academy status, that they think very hard about the implications for their role. If I was not part of a MAT, I would have to buy in an accountancy service, to take on the complicated and detailed requirements in this area.

Our Primary Academy is part of a Multi Academy Trust, which is one business, and registered as one company, with Companies House.

The Trust employs qualified accountancy staff to be responsible for the higher level, detailed production of monthly management and group accounts, and for direct support on a day-to-day basis. The language is different, and the processes more technical, than those we operated before. This for me has been one of the biggest changes and is the area in which I still need support most regularly, but I am learning all the time and feeling more confident with the industry level finance software that we now use.

Overall being an academy has given me a positive experience, wider knowledge and understanding, some big challenges, a roller coaster experience but a fun ride!

3d. Case Study – The Secondary Experience

Peter Beaven, ex-Headteacher of two schools in a Hard Federation, The Midsomer Norton Schools Partnership, describes the importance of the SBM in the Strategic Business Planning process.

Any school needs to plan ahead, identifying the strategic development objectives for the next three to five years; the first year of which will be incorporated into the School Development Plan (SDP) and implemented as the detailed priorities for the academic year.

It was imperative for me to ensure that our Bursar (School Business Manager) played a pivotal role in our strategic development planning as the SDP must be securely underpinned by a business plan setting out the financial implications. This requires a realistic assessment of the school's financial ability to deliver the immediate SDP strategies and project forward to the financial needs of the ensuing years. The current climate of less than generous school funding, underlines the need to have a 'rolling' strategic and financial plan which is based on the most up to date information about funding and local and national circumstances.

How did all of this work in practice?

The 3-5 year Strategic Plan

The Senior Leadership Team would first discuss all known financial changes facing the school over the next three to five years. This would include:

- Looking at demographics and estimating intake numbers and the impact on the budget
- Looking at the staffing profile and estimating changes to staff salary costs, as well as changes to National Insurance and employer's Pension contributions
- Anticipating premises costs for maintenance, refurbishment and development
- Anticipating replacement costs of capital items such as ICT, boilers and other equipment including furniture
- Anticipating changes to funding streams, including known changes to the funding formula, cuts to funding (such as the current cuts to 16+ funding) and the easing of any transitional arrangements
- Anticipating legislative changes such as changes to the curriculum, SEN support etc
- Anticipating the availability of capital monies to be bid for

From this, our Bursar would prepare a 3-5 year budget forecast based on current prices (i.e. not allowing for inflation). This document would be used to inform the school's strategic plan and would be shared with the Finance Committee and, through them, with the full Governing Body.

The Senior Team would then draft a 3-5 year strategic plan. This would be informed by:

- The budget forecasts produced by the Bursar
- Any recent Ofsted Inspection Report
- RAISEonline and other outcome data
- https://www.raisepnline.org/login.aspx?returnUrl=%2f
- The school Self-Evaluation Form
- The school's Vision Statement

- Any information from Governors' committees which highlight future expectations. For example premises development or curriculum change

The Bursar would be fully involved in this process for three major reasons. Firstly, the Bursar would have the best idea about future finances and would be the guardian of financial responsibility and probity. Secondly, the Bursar needs to understand the educational thinking in order to be able to respond adequately when prioritising spending. Thirdly, it is always refreshing and useful to have someone from a different background ask the question "Why do we have to do that?"

Of course, sub-sections of the 3-5 year strategy would include a premises development plan and an ICT strategic plan amongst others.

The draft Strategic Plan would be discussed and amended by governors before approval. This would then be shared with staff.

The School Development Plan (SDP)

The SDP is the planned implementation of the first stage of the Strategic Plan. The Senior Leadership Team would work on this with the Bursar ensuring that the finances could support the plan and that the following issues were not overlooked:

- Problems with cash flow
- Financial risks
- Legal considerations
- HR issues
- Support staff training requirements
- Project management requirements
- Premises issues
- Any need for capital bids
- ICT infrastructure issues
- Procurement and tendering rules

Interlocking plans

From the above it is evident that the school should have strategic objectives over a 3-5 year period; the SDP should support the strategic objectives and be the first phase of implementation.

Any departmental, subject or sectional development plan should support the school priorities and integrate with the SDP. The Bursar would be consulted on these plans, as they too may need to have a budget allocation.

Finally, individual performance management objectives should support the departmental development plan and the SDP. In this way all these processes are interlocked and support each other: there are no contradictions in the system! Furthermore the need to evidence a robust link from performance management to pay progression should be easy to identify.

The current year process

The ongoing implications of the finances against the school plans would be discussed at meetings of the Senior Leadership Team when the Bursar would participate to ensure that the

SDP implementation and the finances are in step.

The Bursar would report to the Head on a fortnightly to monthly basis on the current spend against budget and the cash flow. This would also be reported to the Chair of the Finance Committee.

On a half-termly basis there would be a report from the Bursar to the Finance Committee with the anticipated year-end forecast and an explanation of any variances. Through committee minutes all governors would be made aware of the monitoring process and have an opportunity to debate any key issues arising from unforeseen circumstances.

What is the role of governors?

In my school the governors wanted the Leadership Team to draft the Strategic Plans and the SDP. Governor input came via the committee structure in the drafting stage as governors on the Premises Committee would have their list of priorities, as would the Curriculum Committee. There was an expectation that these would feature in the draft plans.

There was always a robust discussion about the draft plans which governors would thoroughly scrutinise and amend before adopting: in our case this usually took place in the relevant committee.

Summary

One of the key members of the SLT in any school would be the School Business Manager. Without their input at a strategic level any strategic plans may be financially unsound and decisions taken may have unforeseen financial repercussions.

There needs to be a clearly identified route by which governors can evidence their strategic input, discussion, approval and monitoring of the SDP and linked Business Plan.

3e. Business Planning Flow Chart

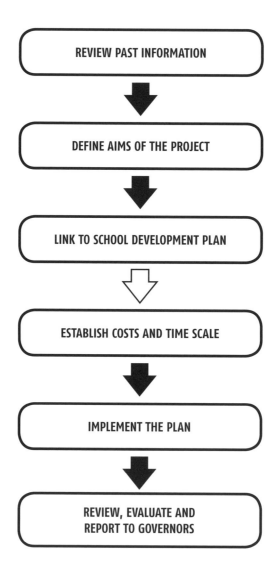

3f. Top Tips for School Business Planning

1. Refer to Section 1 of our Effective Governance guide which explains the role of governors in determining the strategic direction of the school
2. Refer to Section 3.4 of our Effective Governance guide for further case studies showing how the SBM is effectively involved in strategic planning and project delivery
3. Ensure that the SBM is involved in all school improvement strategic planning. This may be best achieved by the SBM being a member of the Senior Leadership Team
4. Ensure that strategic plans and development plans are properly costed
5. Ensure that Financial Projections are drawn up for the next three to five years based on knowledge of demographics, staff profile and any other known factors
6. Align reviews of the SDP, SEF and the budget in order to have the full picture
7. Note that academy conversion aligns the financial and academic years
8. As well as budget planning, keep an eye on cash flow
9. 9Ensure governors are involved in the planning process and feel some ownership of the plans produced

LOCAL ADVICE FOR ACADEMIES FROM SPECIALIST ACCOUNTANTS

The number of academies has increased significantly but that growth has not been without pain as academies face increasing governance, financial and management requirements and restrictions.

Of the many issues facing academies, three are most frequently referenced in discussions with our academy clients, no matter their location. Conversion (either initially or to a Multi Academy Trust), meeting statutory requirements and a squeeze on finances seem to be those playing on the minds of most principals, finance managers and governors.

Some academies are still trying to come to terms with the requirement for monthly management accounting – onerous for busy finance and business managers. And yet whilst such requirements produce challenges, regular accounts enable good management and are essential to good governance.

At the same time, many academies find their financial resources are being squeezed and in consequence may be running down reserves - concerning senior management as well as governors who see budgets that struggle to break even.

There are no easy answers to these issues but the support of a specialist firm of accountants – ideally locally-based – can certainly help with all the requirements and enable development and good management of the schools.

Over the years, we have become recognised as one of the most highly respected accountancy practices working with the education sector – and we have more local offices than any other accountancy practice in the UK. This is important – because no matter how easy communicating electronically has become, having a local partner who is an expert within the field is enormously helpful and reassuring.

Today, we act for more than 50 academies – from small primary schools to MATs (as well as independent fee paying and state funded schools).

Our partners lead experienced teams who understand the challenges and opportunities facing academies, their management and governors. Through liaison with each other, and by exchanging information, we are aware of current and future issues.

Many partners have significant voluntary expertise as school governors and trustees – so are well placed to support executives and boards.

We also believe in providing insight and intelligence. We produce an annual comparison between academies and state/independent schools. Academy clients also receive topical termly 'Alerts' and benefit from seminars and workshops that provide a useful opportunity for governors, principals, bursars and financial managers to network. Recent seminars have included, for instance, guidance on the new Statements of Recommended Practice and monthly management accounts.

There is also meeting the day-to-day requirements before, during and after the conversion process. We help with accounting systems, regulatory returns, maintaining statutory records, give advice on VAT issues, payroll services, benchmarking and overhead reduction – as well as undertaking the statutory audit.

Academies are one of the most exciting areas within education today. Yes, there are challenges – but there is a wealth of expertise to meet those challenges with success.

Henry Briggs
Specialist Charities Partner
Haines Watts

Chapter 4

Financial Procedures – The Audit Process

4a. Introduction

This chapter looks at the role of the School Business Manager in leading the procurement for an auditor and managing the relationship.

Focus of the chapter

Academies have to have an annual external audit. This chapter outlines the process and will be useful for newly converted schools.

The key questions a SBM should think about and governors should ask are:

- Are governors aware that the appointment of an auditor is a governor responsibility?
- How will governors be involved in the process?
- What are the important factors to consider when appointing auditors – educational experience, length of contract etc?
- Is a separate Audit Committee necessary?
- How will the Responsible Officer role be fulfilled?
- How should the SBM, the school and the governors engage with the auditors throughout the year?
- What happens at the annual audit?
- What happens as a result of the management letter?

Context

For some converter academies the annual external audit will be a very different experience from the Local Authority audit. It will be a particularly steep learning curve if the SBM has no experience of managing the school bank account or presenting 'company style' accounts.

It is a governing body responsibility to appoint the auditors, to meet with the auditors to discuss the accounts and their findings and to respond to any issues raised in the ensuing Management Letter. For these reasons, governors should consider whether they have appropriate skills from among their number or whether they should actively seek to make a suitable appointment. These considerations should be addressed early in the conversion process.

Many SBMs find the first academy financial year a challenge, so engaging with the appointed auditors as early as possible after conversion can be a support and resource for determining future good practice.

While there is currently no statutory requirement for a SBM or relevant governor to have an accountancy qualification there is no doubt that many governing bodies are seeking to appoint someone with this qualification. It does highlight the need for the SBM to ensure that they undertake appropriate professional development.

Overview

At the time of going to press there is no statutory requirement for governors to have a separate Audit Committee unless the academy has an income of over £10 million or capitalised assets of over £30 million. Multi Academy Trust structures where the above limits are not breached should consider having a separate Audit Committee. Other academies should identify a committee, usually the Finance Committee, whose remit includes the functions of an Audit Committee.

Academies must also have a process for independent checking of financial controls, systems, transactions and risks. This work may be undertaken by the role of Responsible Officer who would report to the Audit Committee. There are a number of other options for academies to consider to ensure this role is discharged effectively. These include:

- Buying in the expertise from an external provider
- If you engage a large audit firm they might have the ability to offer this service without compromising the audit relationship
- Working in partnership with another academy so that their SBM will undertake the internal controls checks for your school and vice-versa
- Appointment of a non-employed trustee with an appropriate level of qualification as Responsible Officer who will not be paid for the work

It is important that governors have full confidence in the robustness of these internal controls. Many audit firms will supply an annual schedule for the Responsible Officer and will check this as part of their audit. The governors through their Audit or Finance Committee should also undertake a termly scrutiny of the internal controls report.

Check list for appointment of an auditor

This list is not exhaustive but intended to identify key considerations and questions for the governors and SBM.

- Have you identified the potential length of time between conversion and first audit and accounts submission? For example:
  The financial year runs from 1st September to 31st August and accounts must be audited and submitted to the EFA by 31st December. If you convert on 1st January the SBM will have just the 12 months to finalise and submit the accounts whereas a later conversion date, say 1st April means that submission of the first audited accounts may be deferred until 31st December of the following year. Schools need to think carefully about accounts that run for 15 months or more and whether to take up this option

- Prepare your tender document carefully so that it is clear exactly what you are seeking. For example:
  - A firm with experience of the education sector and auditing academies
  - A firm which will support the SBM with interim returns during the first year
  - Any additional services you may want – internal controls, valuation of assets, other accounts e.g. School Fund you want audited at the same time
- Is there a named person who will be your main link with the firm? Is a CV available?
- How are costs apportioned and what travel expenses are to be claimed?
- What additional charges are to be made and on what basis? For example: Any on-going support to the SBM during the first year, any setup and initial review costs?
- What is the fee for the first year and subsequent years?

It is usual for the Audit Committee or a panel of governors from the Finance Committee to interview prospective audit firms and recommend the best option to the governing body for appointment. This meeting is an opportunity for governors to explore how the audit will be conducted and what their role will be as a result of the ensuing Management Letter. While many academies want to encourage a strong working relationship with their auditors it is good practice to re-tender every three years or so and to consider requesting a change of personnel if the same firm is successful.

And finally...

A primary academy SBM suggests a typical annual reporting schedule as follows:

- Monthly report to the Headteacher on income and expenditure since the last meeting. The Chair of the Finance Committee may also be included in this meeting
- Half termly or termly report to Finance Committee including trial balance, bank reconciliation, cash flow report and budget forecast to end of year. It is useful to agree with the Finance Committee and the accountants what they expect as these regular reports
- The Responsible Officer makes a termly visit to undertake internal controls check and the outcome is reported to the next Finance Committee. It is useful to schedule this visit as near a Finance Committee meeting as practical
- In September or October the accountants arrive for about 4 days to produce the annual accounts, which are then audited. In schools where the SBM completes the accounts the auditors will spend some days in school following their audit procedure
- The auditors produce the report to governors in the autumn term and attend the meeting of the Finance Committee where the audit report and Management Letter are discussed. In larger schools it may be the Audit Committee which undertakes this role
- The accounts are presented for governor approval and the response of the school to the auditor's Management Letter reported
- Once approved the accounts are submitted to the EFA by 31st December
- Academies are also required to submit an annual accounts return by 31st January which supports the reparation of consolidated accounts and benchmarking data that is comparable with maintained schools.

4b. Case Study – The Primary Experience

Jo Mercer, School Business Manager of Parbold Douglas CE Academy, Lancashire explains the importance of the audit process for new academies and how to have an effective relationship with the auditors.

Be prepared

School Business Managers are often unaware of how much their role is likely to change as a result of conversion to an academy. There are many new requirements and a completely different reporting timetable placed upon the academy, which were not the case prior to conversion. After conversion the 'rule book' is the Academies Financial Handbook produced by the Education Funding Agency. The expectations placed on the SBM can seem daunting but everything is manageable providing you have the correct information and tools to do the job.

One of the most important decisions the SBM should be involved in is the appointment of auditors. It is my view that this should be considered as soon as possible after conversion and I found it useful to talk to other local SBMs about their experiences with different auditors. Appointing a firm with some knowledge and experience of working in the education sector is very helpful as you want someone who will support you through the first year, identify the reports required and the deadlines to meet.

The Trustees have the formal responsibility to appoint the auditors and they will probably look to you to do the initial procurement work following a good practice procedure before making the decision. The appointment is an annual one and recorded in the Trustee minutes where any subsequent changes will also be minuted. Companies House also need to be informed of any change in auditor.

My advice, once the auditors have been appointed, is to work towards the end of year audit from day one. This should enable you to collate the necessary data as you work through the year and means that the year-end audit is easier for both you and the auditors.

Appointment of an auditor

The process we undertook to appoint the auditor started by me talking to other local academies and then getting quotes from a number of different companies. We followed this up by meeting representatives from each company to tease out and understand exactly what they were proposing and what, if any, additional costs might be charged.

Some companies offer to help you prepare documents during the year at an extra charge and some companies just audit your work at the end of the year. Additional costs need to be planned for and budgeted for if you go down this route. This is an opportunity to identify the skills of the finance team members and plan for any training needs to reduce the additional costs in the future.

Many audit companies recognise that the financial requirements of running a 'business' are new to academies and will offer as much or as little support as you need and will adjust that support in ensuing years. Identifying a company that will do this is the kind of information you should be asking for from other academy SBMs.

As part of the standard service your auditor should be able to give you an annual summary of dates and timescales for Education Funding Agency (EFA) submissions. This is essential to enable you to plan your time to meet these deadlines. In addition your auditor should be in regular contact, perhaps via email, to send you reminders/prompts throughout the year.

Some auditors are proactive and ask for the financial data to be sent to them regularly or they will periodically visit your school to upload the financial data. This can enable them to keep an eye on the data and can ensure they make you aware of any concerns. Other auditors just rely on you keeping your accurate saved records and they will do a full week of scrutiny at year-end.

Although you can change auditors mid-year it is not recommended, perhaps even a little frowned upon! It is however, good practice to go out to tender again approximately every three years. There is no requirement to change the auditing firm but the re-tendering will demonstrate that your decision is made on best value principles.

Impact of academy financial requirements

I found the first year a considerable learning curve. The change of year-end to 31st August means a very different way of working. The busy time is from September to December when a number of governors' meetings and meetings with auditors have to be planned usually escalating towards the end of term. Plan the annual diary and book auditor visit dates as early as possible.

It is crucial to look at what Financial Management System (FMS) you are using or plan to use. I found that the SIMS Financial Management System did not produce everything we required so we investigated other systems such as PS Financials, Carrera and Sage, all of which are used by academies.

As a result of our change of FMS we have adjusted a number of systems to make us more efficient including setting up numerous new ledger codes to scrutinise and monitor the budget in more detail, producing Management Accounts at each period end (each month) and using excel spread sheets for recording our budget monitoring for all activities from staffing forecasts to music lessons. We have also taken on our payroll process and adjusted other Service Level Agreements (SLA) to suit our circumstances and financial year.

Planning, preparation and attention to detail are everything. We are now in a much better position to be able budget, monitor our cash flow which is an important element of academy financial management and plan effectively for the future.

Advice for School Business Managers

I have found the following advice the most helpful in my first year as an academy SBM:

- Do seek recommendations from other local academies before deciding on your new provider if you want to move from the LA as your main service provider for payroll and HR
- Look at all your SLAs in details and break these down into individual ledgers in your budget
- Do join NASBM (National Association of School Business Managers) for support and guidance

- Do join the on-line FD FORUM as this is a supportive network where we help each other with sharing information, policies and answering queries
- Do meet and speak with other academy SBMs at conferences or local groups as again this is a supportive network of sharing best practice, uniting in common cause or discussing policy provisions
- Do undertake the Financial Reporting for Academies short course prior to conversion which will help you manage your time and learning once academy status is achieved
- Do put additional study commitments on hold until you have fully embedded the new academy requirements

And finally...

- Do prioritise well and manage your time effectively
- Do look after your team and keep them well informed about how things are going as they too get familiar with a new timescale and way of working
- Do enjoy the new opportunities and an enhanced status in the school

4c. Sample Terms of Reference for an Audit Committee

The Audit Committee will consider matters relating to internal control and audit. In particular the Committee will:

- Advise the governing body on the adequacy and effectiveness of the Academy Trust's internal control procedures and its arrangements for risk management, control and governance processes
- Advise the governing body on the effectiveness off the Academy Trust's procedures for securing economy, efficiency and value for money
- Monitor the effectiveness of auditors, including the use of auditor performance indicators
- Ensure that any additional service undertaken by the auditors is compatible with the audit independence and objectivity
- Agree and review the work programme of the responsible officer, including the checking of financial controls, systems, transactions and risks
- Consider the reports of the auditors and, when appropriate, advise the governing body of any material control issues
- Monitor the implementation of agreed audit recommendations
- Ensure that all allegations of fraud and irregularity are appropriately investigated and controls weaknesses addressed
- Review the Finance and Estates committee's membership and effectiveness on an annual basis to ensure that it has appropriate skills and relevant experience

The Audit Committee has authority to:

1. Approve responses to audit reports, auditor's management letters, etc
2. Determine the arrangements in respect of the academy's Responsible Officer (R)O) requirements and approve the appointment of RO, or RO related services

4d. Top Tips for Audit Processes

1. Refer to Section 3.4 of our Effective Governance guide for more information about the financial responsibility of governors and the link with the Ofsted framework
2. Refer to Section 6.5 of our Effective Governance guide for more information about financial responsibility of governors when considering or converting to academy status
3. Check the latest requirements about the need for a separate Audit Committee with the EFA
4. Seek recommendations from other local academies before deciding on which firms to invite to tender
5. Engage the auditors before you convert to academy status
6. Make sure your tender document is thorough and covers all the things you want the auditors to do. That way you will not be hit by unexpected costs and the firm appointed will be clear about what is expected of them. This will include:
   a. Any extra support required in the first year of conversion
   b. Training for the Responsible Officer
   c. All the relevant dates for returns
   d. Help with the transfer and valuation of assets
   e. Any other accounts which need auditing
   f. Help with any other returns during the year
   g. The contract period
7. Use the auditors to help you develop good practice at all points of the annual cycle
8. Build up a good relationship with the auditors so that they help you develop best practice
9. Make sure your Financial Management System is fit for purpose

YPO

Delivering savings to schools for forty years

YPO supplies all you need, with a fantastic selection of **27,000 products and 100 service contracts**. From curriculum resources and office supplies, to furniture and facilities management, we provide all you require to successfully run your establishment.

We have been supplying the education sector now for **four decades**. Alongside competitive pricing and free delivery, we also offer a no quibble guarantee on stock items.

Everything in our range is legally complaint with procurement rules and regulations, providing you with protection and the peace of mind that you're getting the best deal. We also provide **free procurement advice and expertise**, and alongside our broad selection and quality, you can rest assured you are saving time, money and resources too.

100% publicly owned, our profits are returned to the public sector – over £105 million to date – for reinvestment in services. Our customers receive a proportion of this annually through our unique loyalty scheme.

YPO was honoured to be declared **Supplier of the Year 2014** at the BESA Education Resources Awards.

Greenhead College realised an instant 10% saving by reviewing their food supply arrangements and accessing the same supplier who was also available through a YPO contract:

"I am delighted with the result. The arrangement is with the same supplier and is almost exactly the same, so without any disruption to the service we have made a substantial saving." *Julie Dyson, Catering Manager – Greenhead College*

Discover more about us and view our range at **www.ypo.co.uk**.

Chapter 5

Procurement – Purchasing Supplies And Services

5a. Introduction

This chapter looks at the role of the School Business Manager in procurement and achieving Value for Money.

Focus of the chapter

This chapter is intended to be a confidence-building chapter for SBMs to deal with procurement compliantly.

Key questions

- What has been the most challenging aspect of procurement for me and how have I resolved this?
- How do I ensure that I achieve value for money?
- How, and for what key decisions, are governors involved in the procurement process?
- How do I monitor and check the internal procurement process with additional school budget holders?
- What have been my successes and what were the key factors in that success?
- How do I work with other schools in or outside any MAT to achieve best value?
- What questions should governors ask at a Finance Committee meeting about procurement?

Context

In 2009 the Audit Commission published its report *'Valuable Lessons'* which examined value for money in school spending. It identified that savings approaching £425m could be achieved if schools procured goods and services more effectively.

The report set out three key principles when considering Value for Money. These were:

- Economy – minimising the cost of goods and services
- Efficiency – the relationship between outputs and the resources used to produce them
- Effectiveness – the extent to which objectives have been achieved

So procurement and value for money is not all about purchasing the cheapest goods or services, but looking at quality and achieving objectives.

The DfE in its June 2013 publication *'Review of efficiency in the schools system'* identified seven key characteristics of the most efficient schools. These included:

- Employing or having access to a skilled school business manager who takes on a leadership role. *This chimes well with our messages in Chapters 1-3*
- Making good use of financial benchmarking information to inform the school's own spending decisions.
- www.educatiuon.gov.uk/sfb/login.aspx
- Making use of school clusters, sharing expertise, experience and data, as well as accessing economies of scale when making shared purchases
- Managing down back office and running costs, as there remains considerable variation in the amount that similar schools spend on running costs, such as energy or premises. The most efficient schools drive these costs down through improved procurement practices and a greater focus on value for money
- Having in place a strong governing body and leadership team that challenges the school's spending

Obviously, the DfE realise that school budgets, although ring-fenced until 2016, face real terms cuts and the need for savings is paramount.

Typically 78-80% of a school budget is spent on staffing, leaving around 20-22% of funds to support the day-to-day operation of the school, covering everything from energy to supplies of pens and paper, ICT to repairs and maintenance, CPD to textbooks. The DfE have introduced Performance Related Pay in 2013 to ensure that value for money is gained from staff costs, to encourage school leaders to not just accept these as set costs. The more value that can be generated from this proportion of funding the more benefit can be delivered to pupils.

Procurement is typically a key responsibility of the SBM. They may not make all the purchases in a large secondary school, but they will have oversight of the budget holders. In addition to ensuring every pound is well spent and achieves value for money, there is also the need to ensure that spending, especially on larger items, complies with all relevant legal aspects attached to school spending. After all, school budgets come from the public purse and schools have the clear responsibility to act with integrity when spending.

The ability to benchmark and compare spending with similar schools is an important tool in improving procurement. The DfE provides access to the Schools Financial Benchmarking website to help with this.

It is wise to ensure you have a comprehensive database of all existing contracts and suppliers. The school may be committed to a number of contracts which may have lengthy periods to run and defined periods of notice for termination. Having this information will help plan ahead.

In cases where the contract is not delivering what it should there is much to be gained from seeking a meeting with the supplier who will typically have an account manager. Effective contract management can quickly bring about improvements in service delivery, changes in prices or specification – don't be afraid to negotiate! Longer contracts can give certainty in setting and planning budgets but may lock you into prices which fall as more suppliers enter the market place, especially if you are dealing with a new service or product.

All purchases should be made in line with school financial procedures which should be documented and available for all staff and governors in the Financial Procedures Manual. The procedures should set out clearly the process to be followed in relation to spending authorisation and spending limits, numbers of quotes and, where necessary, tenders.

Where values exceed the EU tender threshold, schools must comply with European anti-competition legislation and advertise the contract in the European Journal. Failure to follow the correct process may lead to legal challenges from unsuccessful bidders so ensure you seek appropriate advice to avoid any unwanted legal costs. Currently, the thresholds are £111,676 for supplies and services, and £4,322,012 for building works. Obviously, with such high thresholds this may rarely apply to your school!

SBMs should not be afraid to monitor spending by Budget holders to ensure that procedures are being followed and that value for money is being achieved (as well as ensuring budgets are not being overspent).

Increasingly schools are looking to complete procurement on a collaborative basis. Peter Melville explores this in section 5b of this Chapter.

Collaborative procurement can be achieved on a number of levels. At one end of the scale schools may form part of a loose cluster or collaboration whilst at another level they may be part of an academy chain. Either way the purchases are subject to the same criteria that apply if operating on a stand-alone basis. However there are some notable considerations:

- The combined value of the purchase may increase the likelihood of exceeding EU threshold limits especially if you are looking for a 2 or 3-year contract which may be the best option to generate a greater saving
- Agreeing a specification acceptable to all schools may be difficult to achieve especially if the service is complex, such as ICT support, therefore a collaboration on procurement may need to start with something less complicated
- The time commitment invested in managing a collective purchase may outweigh the savings that can be achieved. Careful consideration needs to be given to this at the outset
- There is a risk that a school might pull out of a collective process late in the day which may mean the saving negotiated cannot be delivered. It is therefore important at the start to ensure all those participating are fully committed to the process and understand what this means for their school. Experience shows that it is not uncommon for someone to feel uneasy when it comes to signing the final agreement

If these points can be addressed then there is potential for this to be become a broader strategy for a cluster or chain of schools and deliver savings for the benefit of everyone in the group. *Section 5b looks at Collective Purchasing in more detail.*

The DfE website has advice on procurement in their March 2014 guidance '*Effective buying for your school – For school leaders, school business managers, back office staff and governing bodies in all schools'.* This is part of their extensive section providing guidance on procurement, and is a good source of information and training for SBMs, staff and governors. The website includes access to the Department's 'top ten tips' on procurement – number one being to save time and money by using pre-existing framework agreements which can take much of the hard work and risk associated with procurement away for you. Such advice is very sound when considering purchases such as Photocopiers. There is also much good advice on procuring high value items.

At a national level the DfE is actively looking at the establishment of national frameworks which can be for the benefit of all schools. This has already been seen for copyright licenses and Microsoft products. It is the intention that more national agreements become available so regular monitoring of developments via their web site is a must.

Finally, auditors and governors should sample the procurement process. Obviously, large purchases should be scrutinised by the Finance Committee, checking that any tender process has been complied with and analysing and agreeing which tender should be accepted. This may not be the cheapest, as quality, deliverability, compatibility and timescales are all relevant factors. For smaller purchases they should check that quotes have been received and question the reasons for a quote being successful. This may be done on a sampling basis. They should also question the SBM on how they ensure other budget holders are achieving value for money.

5b. Collaboration for Better Procurement

Peter Melville, School Business Director at William Edwards School, Grays, Essex and creator of Incensu (www.incensu.co.uk) gives an overview of the benefits of collaboration.

Incensu is a register of companies reviewed and rated by the education sector.

Context

Schools should be in control of their finances, but a system in which more and more schools are given the freedom to manage their money has led to many striking out alone when it comes to procurement.

The Department for Education highlighted this issue in its *'Review of efficiency in the schools system'* published at the end of June 2013. It reported that:

> "too many schools continue to procure on their own for goods and services, failing to realise potential economies of scale' adding that 'some areas of school spending could be provided far more cheaply if economies of scale were exploited".

The review highlighted a survey of prices for routine items purchased by all schools (such as ICT equipment and stationery) which showed how costs varied hugely by supplier. The review stated that "many of the items surveyed had a price variance of over 100%, rising to a variance of 966% for one item depending on the supplier selected". Collaboration as a way of sharing resources, experience and expertise is one of several recommendations in the review.

In summer 2013 an Incensu survey discovered that more than 60% of respondents – mainly, SBMs, said they didn't have complete confidence in the buying decisions made by their schools.

Schools achieved best value for money in their buying decisions 'most of the time' according to 78% of respondents, while 8% said that best value for money was 'not always' achieved. Just 14% of respondents could unequivocally say that their school always achieved best value for money in its procurement.

When you look deeper into school spending on an individual school level the picture doesn't get much more encouraging. In our most recent survey of middle leaders in schools we found that the vast majority of spending on stationery and consumables like printer ink was still being made at a departmental level, rather than being part of centralised school purchasing.

If schools work together to purchase services and goods they will have the combined power to get a better deal than the school that goes it alone. As well as more buying power, collaborative purchasing also means that schools can share best practice, knowledge and recommendations about which suppliers to use – and which to avoid.

The challenges of collaboration

Collaboration for better procurement is the ideal but this is still at best patchy around the country. There are a number of reasons for this, including SBMs lacking the time to explore the approach, a desire to keep existing contractors close to them and an uncertainty over the value for money that such an approach will deliver for the school. They may also believe that their approach to procurement may be more effective than the approach used by other schools.

I can understand why some SBMs might be uncertain about the collaborative approach to procurement. When you are in such a highly accountable role it is to be expected that your first impulse might be to play it safe and stay with an approach that you know works.

As a School Business Director (SBD) working in a secondary academy in Essex, I was acutely aware that I had to justify spending decisions to the leadership team and governing body. But I knew that a collaborative approach to procurement offered the best way of delivering best value for my school.

Collaboration with other schools

The first step must be to make that approach. This might be arranging to meet with your opposite in a nearby school over a coffee and talk about your approaches to a specific area, such as grounds maintenance.

Once this step has been taken, you can look at other, more formalised, local bodies that will help you collaborate with other schools. This might include local school business management associations, online forums, as well as consortia. Then there is the national picture, which includes national buying clubs and services.

The main advantage of working with other schools in these various ways is to increase your buying power. But there are other benefits. Sharing and collaborating with other schools increases your professional knowledge and understanding of the pressures faced by schools and SBMs. You will learn the different responses individuals take to these challenge. This will help you in your work and your professional development. Working with other schools also helps you demonstrate to senior leaders and governing bodies that you are exploring every avenue to achieving best value for your school.

Collaboration in procurement saves money at a time when school budgets are under increasing pressure. It also creates new and worthwhile links with new suppliers. I found a fantastic ground maintenance firm which was working with another local school. Now they are working with us as well. I'm now getting better value for money in my grounds maintenance contract than I was before.

Working with suppliers which have already come up to scratch in their school contracts removes a big headache because you don't have to spend as much time tackling issues. You know that this company will do a good job for your school.

Meeting the challenges of collaboration

While collaborating with other schools offers you a wealth of advantages, you also need to be aware of the challenges of this approach.

To begin with, you'll need time and confidence. Most SBMs will need mentoring and support from senior management and reassurance that what they are doing is the right thing.

Working with another school could be a confidence builder rather than something that creates uncertainty. A fellow SBM may well have faced the same challenges and anxieties and will be able to suggest approaches that might work for you as well. An issue shared can be halved.

I can understand why some SBMs might be uncertain about the collaborative approach to procurement. When you are in such a highly accountable role it is to be expected that your first impulse might be to play it safe and stay with an approach that you know works.

As a School Business Director (SBD) working in a secondary academy in Essex, I was acutely aware that I had to justify spending decisions to the leadership team and governing body. But I knew that a collaborative approach to procurement offered the best way of delivering best value for my school.

Collaboration with other schools

The first step must be to make that approach. This might be arranging to meet with your opposite in a nearby school over a coffee and talk about your approaches to a specific area, such as grounds maintenance.

Once this step has been taken, you can look at other, more formalised, local bodies that will help you collaborate with other schools. This might include local school business management associations, online forums, as well as consortia. Then there is the national picture, which includes national buying clubs and services.

The main advantage of working with other schools in these various ways is to increase your buying power. But there are other benefits. Sharing and collaborating with other schools increases your professional knowledge and understanding of the pressures faced by schools and SBMs. You will learn the different responses individuals take to these challenge. This will help you in your work and your professional development. Working with other schools also helps you demonstrate to senior leaders and governing bodies that you are exploring every avenue to achieving best value for your school.

Collaboration in procurement saves money at a time when school budgets are under increasing pressure. It also creates new and worthwhile links with new suppliers. I found a fantastic ground maintenance firm which was working with another local school. Now they are working with us as well. I'm now getting better value for money in my grounds maintenance contract than I was before.

Working with suppliers which have already come up to scratch in their school contracts removes a big headache because you don't have to spend as much time tackling issues. You know that this company will do a good job for your school.

Meeting the challenges of collaboration

While collaborating with other schools offers you a wealth of advantages, you also need to be aware of the challenges of this approach.

To begin with, you'll need time and confidence. Most SBMs will need mentoring and support from senior management and reassurance that what they are doing is the right thing.

Working with another school could be a confidence builder rather than something that creates uncertainty. A fellow SBM may well have faced the same challenges and anxieties and will be able to suggest approaches that might work for you as well. An issue shared can be halved.

Persistence is another quality that is needed, especially when time is an issue. You may need to dedicate two to three hours a week to sit down and look at what contracts you have and assess whether they are offering you best value and, if not, what you should do about them. Try to be disciplined about it and work through your contracts book on a week-by-week basis.

Changing the status quo can often be difficult especially when a supplier has worked for your school for a long time. You have to be prepared to cut ties if that contract is not delivering best value. But it may also be that the contract is exactly what you need. Be prepared to judge every contract by the same criteria. It can be reassuring to know that an established contract has passed the same test that is applied to new or prospective contracts.

And finally...

I believe that it is a good thing that schools are increasingly in control of their budgets and the SBM has a real input into the strategic ethos of the school. By schools working together developing the confidence to engage in a shared strategic vision we can ensure that the collaborative approach will deliver the best value for our schools and our pupils.

5c. Achieving Value for Money

There are many ways for schools to achieve value for money when purchasing goods and services.

FASNA Members have listed many basic ideas which may be of interest such as:

- Be prepared to shop around and negotiate with suppliers when existing contracts are about to end. This applies to energy firms, photocopy providers, ICT providers and any lease, service level agreements or contracts you have
- Be prepared to shop around and negotiate with current suppliers for other purchases, especially furniture, carpets, equipment and larger amounts of stationary and supplies
- Collaborate with other schools to increase the bulk purchase and maximize price reduction
- Be prepared to negotiate with successful bidders on capital items which have been tendered for- this can achieve savings
- Group your school purchases to maximize economies of scale rather than let departments, key stages or individual teachers order their supplies separately. For example, this might mean imposing a standard exercise book across the school
- Stock check regularly – especially in primary schools – there will be surplus material which can be redistributed or not reordered
- Ensure the costs of photocopying are charged to cost centres. It teaches staff to use the facility responsibly and re-use copies where possible
- Look carefully at Local Authority Service Level Agreements. Do they deliver what you want? Is the quality right? Are they good value for money? Can you buy the service elsewhere for a better price – and maybe a better quality?
- Check that ICT software is actually being used. Do this by analysis of use. Too often licenses are bought when a product excites a member of staff and actual use tails off but no one cancels the license payment
- Investigate whether materials for art and technology can be donated rather than bought. Many companies will throw away material which might be used in schools such as card, paper, cloth, wood and metal
- Explore buying on-line (for which you need a school credit card). This can save money

There are many such ideas and we cannot be exhaustive.

Here are some specific Case Studies to illustrate the issue.

5d. Case Studies – Examples of Better Procurement

Two examples of the benefits of collaborating across more than one school:

Debi Markham – Business Manager, Witham St Hughs Academy, Lincoln

About 2 years ago I was involved in setting up a cluster group of local primary schools around the area. Some of these schools are academies but most are still part of the Local Authority (this makes no difference to any of us as we all work together). This cluster group has become very successful and now has fifteen members. We write our own agenda and invite businesses and organisations to come along to the meetings to discuss the services that they offer. As a result of this, we have been able to obtain many cluster discounts including grounds maintenance, staff sickness insurance, ICT provision, Supply Agency discounts, coach hire and stationery orders. We hold the meetings away from the school at a local venue and each pay £30 per year to become a member, which covers the hire of the venue and tea/coffee and biscuits.

Now we are finding that organisations are approaching us to come to the meetings and the meetings are packed with information. We also use these meetings to discuss issues that have arisen from companies we are using with representatives from the cluster group, meeting with the organisation to iron out any problems. It has proved to be a good bargaining tool as they are acutely aware that there is the potential to lose several schools rather than just one and we have found the concerns are addressed quickly.

We have kept the group to a small, manageable size to ensure that the meetings are relevant to most of the members. We also have a group email, which is regularly used to just ask questions or for general information. This has proven to be a quick easy way of resolving something when we are all very busy.

Andrew Joyce, Head of Finance - Cabot Learning Federation, Bristol

By identifying major areas of expenditure and reviewing the suppliers we use across the Federation, we have been able to make useful savings. Having provided evidence to the supplier of our spend levels, we were able to enter into negotiations to receive discounts for all our academies. With one particular supplier, we were able to negotiate a 10% discount, which generated savings in the region of £10–£15k per annum.

Five examples of cost saving in single schools:

Richard Barnard, Chair of Governors, Robinswood Primary Academy, Gloucester

A good example of effective financial management and value for money is our constant review of costs and contracts in relation to the in-house meals provision. For a number of years this has enabled us not only to keep charges to our parents at least 10p and often 20p below that charged by the LA contractor but also provide healthy fresh meals with many supplies locally sourced.

Lorraine Knight, School Business Manager, Baschurch CE Primary School, Shrewsbury

We are a rural village state maintained primary school in Shropshire.

Firstly, we have saved £4000 per annum by taking our catering in-house instead of using the

County catering provider. We are using a management company, Watson Lennard & Payne to ensure we meet nutritional guidelines. They will also provide training and a procurement service. By having the opportunity to choose our own menu we hope to increase the uptake too. The kitchen staff now feel empowered and are rising to the challenge.

Secondly, by using a neighbouring Local Authority's ICT service team instead of our Local Authority's preferred supplier to replace our wireless network, we have saved £3500. Although it is not a totally like-for-like system, we are more than confident that it will meet our needs.

Lynn Marshall, Bursar, Hartwell Primary School, Northamptonshire

We reviewed our Absence/Maternity Insurance, changed suppliers and achieved a saving on the premium of £2239.

To facilitate the review I sent an 'all bursars' email to all the schools in my County asking for recommendations for companies and their contacts and costs. It took a bit of time but was well worth the final outcome. This process is used regularly to ascertain best value on a variety of services and products.

Jo Seymour, Headteacher, St Peter and Paul's Primary, Bromley, Kent

We had a paint amnesty, with everyone's supply being put on tables in the hall. This revealed excessive bottles of black and no red or orange! Once equitably redistributed and the necessary missing colours bought, the impact was staff knowledge, trust and understanding of the budget situation, and even more importantly the correct tools to do the job. Why did we even have so much black paint?

Similarly, we had a purple paper crisis before Lent – we need it for the Liturgical displays but where did it all go? Having to spend an extra £50 on backing paper was a problem. Then

Mr H made an appearance "Well, it's in my cupboard. I thought if I kept it, I knew it would be safe and we would have it for when we needed it". It all adds up. How much money do you have banked in the cupboards? And who knows where these things are? A good argument for a regular 'amnesty', 'cupboard open afternoon' or SBM stock check.

Savings made by moving from Local Authority provision

Eileen O'Dwyer, School Business Manager, William Tyndale School, Islington

Cleaning Contract: The main saving the school has made is changing the cleaning contract. For years we had been with the Local Authority who then moved the contract to a private contractor. Not only was the contract extremely expensive but the quality of the cleaning was appalling.

The school entered the tendering process and appointed a cleaning company that is employed by the Queen to clean Windsor Castle and Buckingham Palace. The contract was £10,000 cheaper a year. It was onerous to change the contract and two of the staff had to be TUPED across but it has been very beneficial to the school both financially and in the increased quality of cleaning.

I negotiate on every contract and purchase and am always given a discount. In these difficult times companies will compromise on price. I use contractors who give excellent value for money and fantastic workmanship. I wanted a trophy cupboard and it was going to cost £3500 from a catalogue. I had a bespoke cabinet made from hardwood with lighting which cost £2500.

Legal Services contract: Even though this contract was cheaper with the Borough, the actual service was inadequate. The school now has a contract with solicitors who answer any query within a day. If the matter is more complicated the company keeps the school informed of progress.

Speech and Language Consultant: This service was supplied via the borough but different people were sent and if the consultant was ill the time was not made up. We have arranged for an independent consultant to visit three times a week and we pay her directly. She has built up excellent relationships with both the children and staff and has become an invaluable part of the team.

5e. Top Tips for Procurement – Purchasing Supplies and Services

1. Refer to Sections 3.4.1, 3.4.2 and 3.4.4 of our Effective Governance guide for more information about the overarching financial responsibility of governors including monitoring financial procedures and practice and benchmarking
2. Use benchmarking data where available, in order to compare spending
3. Speak to other schools about what they are paying for services, contracts and supplies
4. Look for ways to work with other schools on purchasing to maximise cost benefits
5. School Business Managers should monitor budget holders spending and intervene to achieve best value
6. Ensure the Financial Procedures Manual is clear on spending authorisations and ensure these are followed
7. Don't be afraid to negotiate on price
8. Check any Service Level Agreements with the Local Authority (or any other provider) to ensure you are getting what you want and what you pay for
9. Explore buying on-line (for which you need a school credit card)
10. Check ICT software licenses and only renew those actually being well used
11. Look at the Procurement section of the DfE website
12. Develop a Procurement Policy

Chapter 6

Premises And Facilities Management

6a. Introduction

This chapter looks at the additional elements of the School Business Manager role relating to premises and facilities management and reminds governors of their role in supporting this.

Focus of the chapter

To consider the skills and qualities demanded of a SBM taking charge of managing premises – especially as many elements of this role may well be a new addition to the role for a primary SBM.

Key questions:

- What are the main criteria in your job description which relate to premises and facilities management?
- What training did you undertake in preparation for this role?
- Do you have any line management responsibilities relating to this role?
- How do you ensure effective Health and Safety (H&S) awareness amongst staff and governors?
- What role does the governing body play in policy determination in this area?
- What are the responsibilities of the governing body in this area?
- What were the most challenging aspects of the role to start with and how did you ensure success?
- What are the key actions you undertake on a termly and annual basis to ensure that appropriate plans e.g. the asset management plan and risk register are relevant and reflect the needs of the school?

Overview

The role and status of the SBM has developed and expanded in many schools to include responsibility for premises and facilities management. For example, at one end of the scale this may be an overview and line management role of a separate Business Development Manager or Site Manager, who have the direct responsibility for site staff and cleaners. At the other end of the scale this might be the expectation that the SBM will have a more 'hands on' role and take direct responsibility for cleaners, caretakers, catering staff, grounds maintenance arrangements etc.

Responsibility for many aspects of good premises management has been delegated to all schools over a period of time by Local Authorities. For example, the regular inspection of electrical equipment, water storage tanks for legionella, asbestos registers and fire safety procedures will simply have to continue in much the same way. On conversion to academy status some contracts may have to be changed or re-negotiated when the term ends and governors need to recognise that the ultimate responsibility for these elements now resides with the governing body. Many academies will continue to buy this service from the Local Authority but there are other providers who can do this for schools.

Health and safety

For governors this is often a cause for concern. A nominated governor to link with the school for the purposes of health and safety monitoring could be useful in evidencing governors' understanding and effectiveness. This need not be an onerous task but could include an annual inspection of the staff handbook to verify induction and on-going training, school logs identifying incident reports, risk assessments for residential school trips and regular checks on systems and equipment. It might also involve periodic health and safety checks of the school buildings with the caretaker or the site team.

Schools may also have a Trade Union Health and Safety representative who needs to be involved in the monitoring of health and safety.

The DfE document *Health and safety: Advice on legal duties and powers - For local authorities, school leaders, school staff and governing bodies* updated in February 2014 states:

> "Health and safety law requires the employer to assess the risks to the health and safety of staff and others affected by their activities. The terms risk assessment and risk management are used to describe the process of thinking about the risks of any activity and the steps taken to counter them.
>
> Sensible management of risk does not mean that a separate written risk assessment is required for every activity. School employers should always take a common sense and proportionate approach, remembering that in schools risk assessment and risk management are tools to enable children to undertake activities safely, and not prevent activities from taking place. Sensible risk management cannot remove risk altogether but it should avoid needless or unhelpful paperwork.
>
> Some activities, especially those happening away from school, can involve higher levels of risk. If these are annual or infrequent activities, a review of an existing assessment may be all that is needed. If it is a new activity, a specific assessment of significant risks must be carried out. Headteachers should ensure that the person assigned with the assessment task understands the risks and is familiar with the activity that is planned. Where a risk assessment is carried out the employer must record the significant findings of the assessment.
>
> However, schools need not carry out a risk assessment every time they undertake an activity that usually forms part of the school day, for example,

taking pupils to a local venue which it frequently visits, such as a swimming pool, park, or place of worship. Any risks of these routine activities should already have been considered when agreeing the school's general health and safety policies and procedures. A regular check to make sure the precautions remain suitable is all that is required."

It is useful to remind governors that health and safety is more about effective risk identification and risk management than it is about throwing money at a problem to 'solve' it as quickly as possible. Forward planning in terms of accurate condition assessments of premises and good budget information can go a long way to mitigating 'nasty' surprises to do with the buildings and land.

As far as student and staff welfare is concerned, governors need to ensure that all the required systems are in place with regard to vetting and that there are appropriate policies and staff training for child protection, first aid, school activities etc. The important point here is that governors can evidence that these procedures are effective either through a governor link and/ or through regular updates and log scrutiny by a committee.

Whereas the SBM usually has responsibility for the health and safety issues to do with premises and probably external contractors, it may not be part of the role to ensure that the personnel element of health and safety is functioning well. However encouraging governors to understand the duality of the role is helpful.

Managing buildings and premises

The SBM may have oversight of the Site Team. In a small school this might just be the caretaker. The key issue here is ensuring that their work is logged to ensure that best use is being made of their time and skills. Care needs to be taken that they are trained to do the tasks you want them to do and that their health and safety is protected.

With cleaning, there needs to be a process of checking the quality if cleaning and that cleaners are working efficiently and effectively. In a large school this may be done through a Head Cleaner or Cleaning Manager. Care needs to be taken that cleaning equipment is correctly used and properly maintained and that cleaning products and are correctly used and stored. Purchases in this area should also be monitored for value for money.

The SBM may also be involved in monitoring the school buildings. There are four areas here: maintenance, repair, refurbishment and replacement. An annual Condition Survey carried out by the governors with some external support may help inform the annual cycle of repair and refurbishment. This needs to be budgeted for. This may also help support any bid for capital money for buildings in poor condition, where condition is impacting on provision and outcomes, or a potential health and safety risk.

Governors also need to discuss Basic Need – the sufficiency of the accommodation to deliver the curriculum to the numbers of pupils on roll. This may also lead to a capital bid being made. (*See Chapter 7 for information on Bid Writing*).

The use of an architect to help develop a bid, or to oversee the work carried out if a bid is successful might be an advantage.

Of course, there may also be the need for the SBM to oversee the work of contractors. At the outset, this might be the contract tender process, then monitoring the delivery of the contract. These may be building contractors carrying out work in the school – large or small projects, grounds maintenance contractors, cleaning contractors, window cleaners, ICT installation contractors and so on.

In all of this, the relevant Governors Committee is crucially important. It is a good idea to have some premises expertise on this committee. In the next section, we look at the role of governors and how Ofsted might judge the governance of premises.

Our case studies then look at the SBM's role from both a primary and secondary perspective.

6b. Governance and Ofsted

In this section we look at the Ofsted framework (2012) and what they expect a school to be doing with regard to premises.

Note that in August 2014 the DfE streamlined Ofsted guidance. Details can be found at www.ofsted.gov.uk/resources/school-inspection-handbook

Governors will support the role of the SBM with regard to premises if they fulfil their responsibilities well.

In a well-governed school or academy the following features should be in place:

- Premises matters being the remit of a committee with clear terms of reference and identification of delegated powers
- Some Governors having a deeper understanding of premises issues
- Governors being aware of health and safety responsibilities
- Appropriate arrangements in place for the maintenance and upkeep of the buildings and grounds
- There will be an appropriate reporting cycle to the full Governing Body from the Committee dealing with premises

According to the Inspection Framework, when a school or academy is inspected the Inspectors should consider how well governors:

- Ensure..... resources (and this includes physical resources) made available to the school are managed effectively
- Ensure that all pupils are safe

and consider:

- The promotion of safe practices and a culture of safety, including e-safety

Governors need to ask themselves the following questions:

1. Are there appropriate health and safety policies and procedures in place?

   The responsibility for health and safety rests with the employer. Governors need to ensure that the school has appropriate health and safety policies and procedures relating to premises, which will include:

   - Fire safety – when were the premises last checked for fire safety? Have there been regular recorded fire drills? Have evacuation procedures been clearly signed and do pupils and staff know what to do? Are fire extinguishers appropriately distributed, with clear signage and evidence of being checked? Are fire doors appropriately installed and fire exits signposted? These are some of the basics governors need to ensure are in place. The local fire officer can help check these
   - Is there a policy about electrical equipment and are Portable Appliance Tests (PAT tests) carried out as required?
   - Is there a policy for carrying out tests for legionella and are these recorded and reported?

- Is here an asbestos register?
- If any work to buildings is carried out is there a check for asbestos contamination?
- Does the school have a process for reporting health and safety concerns? If so, what happens once they are reported?
- Are risk assessments carried out for activities inside and outside the classroom?
- Is there are a clear policy covering who is responsible for carrying out these risk assessments and for how they are recorded?
- What about COSSH (Control of Substances Hazardous to Health) regulations? Are the science staff, the cleaning staff and site team all aware of these and properly trained? Are records properly kept?
- Have governors seen the DfE document – *Health and safety: Advice on legal duties and powers – For local authorities, school leaders, school staff and governing bodies* updated in February 2014?

Governors need to ensure that there is an effective reporting process to a governing body committee on these issues. Health and safety matters relate to both personnel and premises areas so it needs to be clear where responsibilities lie in the terms of reference for governors committees. For example, which committee has responsibility for oversight of health and safety on school trips? What about health and safety in science, technology and PE lessons? Whilst the school policy should make it clear which members of staff are responsible in these areas it may need to be clarified which Governor Committee has oversight. It may be more obvious which committee has responsibility for premises health and safety.

Are lines of responsibility and accounting clear and well known? The role of the SBM needs to be clear and the SBM needs to be supported in ensuring they have the skills and training for what is expected of them.

2. How do governors undertake their responsibility for health and safety of pupils, staff and others visiting or using the school?
3. How secure is the site, e.g. are there appropriate door mechanisms to main entrances and is the boundary of the site secure?
4. How is the security of pupils and staff managed, e.g. what process do visitors have to go through to gain access?

Here governors need to be reassured that there is a process for screening visitors which cannot be bypassed and that the site cannot be accessed without going through the screening process. Besides the process of screening, governors may need to consider how the entrance and reception area works and how the site boundary is made secure.

5. What is the percentage of the school budget allocated to maintenance or refurbishment projects?
6. Who is responsible for monitoring the condition of the school premises and grounds?

Each year there should be a budget to ensure that essential remedial health and safety work can be carried out. There may also be a programme of repairs and refurbishment, which are identified and budgeted for. Whilst oversight of this may lie with a Premises Committee it could be that the responsibility for overseeing premises issues may be incorporated into the remit of the Finance Committee. Whichever committee has the responsibility, financial regulations should identify the tender process to be followed if a project is likely to cost over an agreed sum.

Schools may have their own site teams or may contract out this service. Governors should check that there is a process by which the condition of the buildings and grounds is monitored and remedial work or refurbishment incorporated into the budget. If a service is contracted out there should be an identified individual in school responsible for managing the contract.

7. How do governors ensure that the physical environment of the school supports learning?
8. How are improvements incorporated into the school plans and budget?
9. What is the impact of any PFI or BSF agreement on the budget?

Here there needs to be linkage between Committees. Does the Curriculum Committee, or the committee with responsibility for learning and outcomes, have a process by which recommendations can be made to the Premises Committee and then to the Finance Committee? Is there a clear and systematic process which links this up?

If there is a PFI or BSF agreement, who monitors it and reports on its effectiveness?

Finally, the key responsibilities of the Chair of Governors for premises are to ensure that:

- Premises matters are within the remit of a committee reporting regularly to the full governing body meetings
- Non-premises health and safety issues have a clear line of accountability and reporting to the appropriate committee
- There is an effective process for monitoring and consideration of health and safety matters
- Appropriate security arrangements are in place and monitored on a regular basis
- The condition of school buildings and grounds is managed effectively
- The SBM is well supported and capable of undertaking these responsibilities.

6c. Case Study – The Primary Experience (1)

Kathy Haig, School Business Manager of Cooper's Edge, a two form entry Primary School in Brockworth, Gloucestershire, identifies the principles of premises and facilities management and describes her role in ensuring effective implementation.

Overview

Schools vary in size, shape, age and condition, but a key principle of effective premises and facilities management – the responsibility for the health and safety of all staff, pupils and users of the facilities applies to them all.

The Health and Safety at Work Act 1974 places overall responsibility for health and safety with the employer. Who this is varies with the type of school. For example, for the various types of community schools, the employer is the Local Authority (LA), for foundation schools and voluntary aided schools the employer is the governing body, for academies the employer is the Academy Trust. The employer has the overall strategic responsibility and the Headteacher or Principal will have responsibility for the implementation of protocols, practice and relevant policies while the SBM may have responsibility for the day-to-day management of the school procedures.

Health and safety covers a raft of issues including school trips and activities, the use of specialist equipment, car parking arrangements and first aid procedures. The important element is evidence of an appropriate risk assessment, which notes any actions to be taken as a result of this. The risk assessment needs to be proportionate to the activity and a general assessment may cover a range of regular activities such as trips to local venues.

Governor and staff responsibilities

Effective health and safety arrangements depend on governor and staff awareness of their responsibilities and duty to comply with school policies. To ensure this responsibility is disseminated to all staff I complete an induction session with new staff before they commence work in the school and arrange regular refresher sessions for longer serving staff. The sessions include direct reference to the Health and Safety Policy and other related school policies. It is important that staff have their own copies in the staff handbook or equivalent or know where to access a copy on the school IT network for example.

The policies very clearly identify the responsibility of staff when working on the premises, and include information about pupil/staff ratios for offsite visits to protocols of drinking hot drinks in the classrooms. Some schools in rural areas include a policy about working alone in the school during evenings and/or weekends.

Governors are made aware of their responsibilities through the governors' committee structure and governor training sessions. It is important that governors are able to evidence their role in ensuring that appropriate risk assessment checks are undertaken and recorded through committee minutes. In some schools a governor will undertake an assessment walk with the Headteacher or Site Manager to identify any potential risks or a small group of governors may undertake an annual audit of the premises to ensure that the school is a safe place for the pupils, staff and visitors. Good practice suggests that a termly assessment walk by the

Headteacher or Site Manager with a different governor each time to provide the fresh pair of eyes is a reasonable model to follow.

Strategic development

Strategically, governors must ensure that their premises and facilities management policies are directly linked to supporting the school in its drive for improvement. Through formal and informal discussions they can influence the ethos and strategic development of the school in many ways.

When I managed a small, rural school that was over 150 years old, the governors had the oversight of many building projects from kitchen renovations to the refurbishment of the playground. Whilst I ensured that the projects complied with health and safety legislation and were delivered within budget, the governors ensured that the works were in keeping with the style and character of the original building. This enhanced the overall position of the school in the local community and helped to foster a positive relationship between the school and the community.

In my current school, which is less than three years old, the governors have ensured that maximum use is being made of school premises by developing a lettings policy that complies with the philosophy of the school as a 'community based school used by the community', which in turn helps to secure a sustainable revenue stream. Rooms are hired for a wide range of activities such as birthday parties, meetings of clubs and societies, one off celebration events, youth activities etc.

Operational matters

School buildings vary considerably and older buildings particularly present their own challenges. My first school had a quirky heating system, hard to locate gas and electricity meters and hidden stopcocks, the location of which nobody could remember during emergency situations.

My new school building has high tech, computerised plant rooms and electronic building management systems accompanied by a shelf full of documentation on how to operate all aspects of the school, down to the light switches! My site manager is currently in the process of condensing the information into a 'basic guide' so that the important information can be easily understood and actioned in an appropriate way by staff.

The management of school premises can be challenging and it is important to ensure that school procedures are well documented and well communicated and that routine inspections and checks of equipment and services are undertaken.

For example, I ensure that water temperatures are taken on a monthly basis and that Portable Appliance Testing is undertaken on an annual basis. My site manager currently records this information on a simple spreadsheet records the dates and finding of the checks and what action if any has been completed to ensure compliance with legislation. This document can easily be accessed by me and the Headteacher to monitor that required checks have been done and are then reported to an appropriate governing body committee.

There are many companies now who will provide a service to ensure the school is compliant with current legislation for all these checks and tests. One of my responsibilities is to ensure contractors that are engaged to undertake annual inspections such as lighting and boiler maintenance, will provide us with 'best value', are accredited to undertake the tasks and are also willing to engage actively with the management of the school so that they too become familiar with its functionality.

A good working relationship with a local firm can be invaluable when dealing with emergency issues such as the loss of heating or gas before a major event! An important element of these routine tasks is to keep up to date so that I can recommend appropriate changes to school policies and practices and ensure that governors are also informed.

Professional development

When I started as a School Business Manager in a two-form entry primary school I was supported in my responsibility for premises management by the Site Manager. Neither of us entered our professions with formal training for undertaking our responsibilities!

Initially I undertook premises training, which was aimed at Headteachers and staff with premises management responsibilities, provided by the Local Authority. This gave me the latest legislative responsibilities that I had to undertake for our school premises.

I still access advice and support throughout the year from the Property Services Team at our Local Authority. This is a service that we purchase on an annual basis through our Traded Service options. My knowledge has also increased through studying the CSBM qualification. On a local level I ensure that my knowledge is kept up to date by attending seminars provided by the Gloucestershire Association of School Business Mangers (GASBM) as well as keeping up to date by reading publications provided by organisations such as FASNA and NASBM.

Being an integral part of the school leadership focused on ensuring that the premises are supporting school improvement and offering opportunities to the community is a rewarding job and one which continues to develop.

6d. Case Study – The Primary Experience (2)

Gaylene Saunders, School Business Manager of Farndon Fields, a primary academy of 195 pupils in Market Harborough, Leicestershire, explains how she organised premises and facilities management after conversion to an academy.

Context

Farndon Fields Primary School is a medium-sized primary academy with 195 pupils. We are growing in numbers as a result of a new housing development in our catchment and have recently had a new two-classroom extension completed. We converted to academy status in July 2012 in a collaborative partnership with four other primary schools in our area (the Harborough Collaborative Trust). We retain autonomy as an academy and as part of the collaborative trust are formalising and developing the existing links between our schools in a more structured way.

Impact of academy status

As a maintained school, we barely noticed the various companies that turned up to carry out numerous annual maintenance requirements, and if anything needed fixing then it was a simple matter of calling the Local Authority Property Helpdesk.

After conversion it hit home that the 'safety net' of the Local Authority was no longer there. In the brave new world of operating as an academy, premises and facilities management becomes an important and time-consuming area that requires careful planning and co-ordination.

The realisation came to me, however, that the network of colleagues that I had been collaborating with long before 'collaboration' became the buzz word of the moment, were still there as my support network. There were many other sources of information and help that I could tap into such as the Financial Directors Forum (FDF), Freedom and Autonomy for Schools National Association (FASNA), National Association of School Business Managers (NASBM), National College for Teaching and Leadership (NCTL), Education Funding Agency (EFA) and of course, appropriate advice from the local authority services that we bought back into.

The local authority quickly adapted itself to 'sell' to academies. Some of the services that were sold back to academies were very effective and worthwhile, however we decided not to buy back into the service to assist with premises management as we agreed that this was not robust and not good value for money.

Staffing challenges and successes

First of all I carried out a SWOT analysis of the premises staff, which highlighted strengths in the areas of maintenance of buildings and grounds and carrying out small building alterations. Having a team competent to carry out these jobs saves the school a significant amount of money. Weaknesses highlighted were based around paperwork and recording health and safety checks. Record keeping in these areas is important so that the regular weekly, monthly or termly health and safety checks are clearly identified as completed, any risks recognised and appropriate action taken or planned.

I believe there is great value to be had in playing to people's strengths, therefore decided to put in place additional provision to counteract the 'weaknesses'. We appointed a Health and Safety Assistant to work two hours a week on health and safety checks, risk assessments, and any other related tasks as required. This has worked really well and the paperwork is now in place and checks are regularly done and documented.

Cyclical maintenance plan

Identifying what was happening as a Local Authority school and what should be taking place involved considerable research before we could begin to construct a suitable annual plan. Historical information of when maintenance visits had taken place as well as information given to us by our health and safety advisor helped us to construct a timetable.

Support from the Local Authority Health & Safety Department (which we bought back into) is excellent and our allocated advisor regularly visits to go through relevant issues and the measures we should have in place. Focused information and advice from them is integral to the development of a robust premises management plan and has, for example, highlighted the fact that the government is currently scrutinising the management of asbestos in academies.

Through our research we discovered that we needed an annual test of our lightning rod which had never happened before because the Local Authority was apparently unaware that we had a lightning rod! This reinforces the message that the people best placed to maintain and manage the building (and of course receive the funding direct to do this) are the school staff.

To support our cyclical maintenance plans we have compiled a list of contractors in collaboration with other schools who have provided recommendations. It is good to be able to support local people with the work where previously local authority contractors travelled from miles away. This supports our ethos as a 'green' school.

The role of the School Business Manager

The level of involvement that the SBM has in the day-to-day management of premises is dependent upon the size of the school and the competency of premises staff. The role of the SBM in premises matters ranges from a very operational role to one that is solely strategic. I have a colleague who is in a small school and she has a very 'hands on' role, as there are fewer premises staff with limited experience and technical skill.

Having a full time premises officer or site director enables the SBM to be more strategic and delegate responsibility for routine maintenance tasks while having overall responsibility for ensuring that quotations for checks are obtained and the checks completed and recorded.

I sit somewhere in the middle, with my role including an amount of operational premises management, such as liaising with contractors when there is a maintenance requirement, and obtaining quotations and managing capital projects.

The part of my role that gives me great satisfaction is the strategic premises management and development. Putting together the Premises Development Plan and thinking about future development of the premises and where we might enhance the learning environment opens up exciting opportunities. Creative thinking comes to the fore, and as a result, we are developing part of our large playing field into an allotment garden as a facility which can be used by the community. The facility can also be used by the children to learn gardening techniques, and to grow fresh vegetables that can be used in the school kitchen. Having a good team in place makes it very easy to achieve innovative plans.

Another important part of my role as an academy SBM is income generation. This is linked with management of the premises as promoting and developing lettings opportunities is a good regular source of income.

I also receive regular updates from the EFA website regarding opportunities to apply for Academies Capital Maintenance Fund (ACMF) grants. I have been successful in gaining two grants from this fund – one to replace the school's windows and doors (no more draughty single glazed windows ensure we keep the heating we pay for in the school) and another to enhance the security of the school.

It is important that staff are actively involved in ensuring the premises are safe and fit for purpose as well as engaging them in the development of the premises. Part of my line management of premises, administration and kitchen staff involves holding a weekly 'catch up' meeting to ensure that staff are informed of what is happening in school during the week and enabling them to raise any maintenance or health and safety issues to be addressed.

Important policies and plans

I found that I needed to be clever in the way I worked given the significant time pressures following conversion and embraced the 'why reinvent the wheel' attitude.

The list of policies required is daunting but there are a number of places and organisations from which to get help. Our health and safety advisors supplied us with a number of model policies which were an excellent starting point from which to develop policies customised and relevant to our school. NASBM also has a number of model policies and my local school business manager network was a really useful source of information too.

Having a Disaster Recovery and Business Continuity Plan (DRBCP) is crucial to academies. Insurers will want to know that you have this document in place. It is important to think of the academy as a business where the children and parents are the 'clients'.

There are several scenarios that will need to be covered in the DRBCP, take for instance the worst-case scenario – the school burns down. If we cannot put alternative arrangements in place quickly to ensure continued provision for our 'clients' then we may lose their custom; i.e. they are placed in another school while the building is being rebuilt and just never make the move back to our school. Loss of clients means loss of income and the academy could find itself in a difficult financial situation.

Health and safety awareness is another hugely important area of premises management. Ensuring the safety of pupils and staff is vital and it is the policies and procedures that, we as a school, put in place that will make sure the school environment is a safe place to be. It is important that all staff are fully aware of their individual responsibility for health and safety through induction, school policies and regular updates. Access to good advice and support is important and we receive excellent support from our health and safety advisors. The Health and Safety Executive (HSE) is another good source of information providing guidance documents, sample risk assessments, legislative updates etc.

Responsibilities of the Governing Body

In an academy the ultimate responsibility for health and safety compliance lies usually with the governing body, so it is important that they have a robust system of risk assessment and oversight.

Our committee with responsibility for premises management is the Safeguarding, Facilities and Estates (SAFE) Committee. Strong committee structures and timely committee and governing body meetings, combined with a timetable of well-planned governor visits ensures that development and ratification of policies and procedures is effective. This supports the management and development of the premises and enables full health and safety compliance. Governor training is focussed to support this area of responsibility. Governor health and safety visits take place twice a year and other governor visit focuses include: the Risk Register, the Disclosure and Barring Service Child Protection register (DRBCP), risk assessments and fire evacuation procedures.

Key actions – this is a summary of my schedule

Termly

- Health and safety checks – ensure that weekly and monthly fire and legionella tests are being carried out and recorded
- Risk assessment updates as required – Control of Substances Hazardous to Health Regulations (COSHH), trips, building etc
- Analysis of training requirements
- Fire practices and assessments of any weak areas – amend the fire procedures if necessary
- Risk Register – this is revisited at each SAFE Committee meeting and updated if necessary

Annual

- Health and safety audit – our health and safety advisors attend and carry out an audit, producing a report which is presented to the SAFE committee. The Action Plan from this audit is included in the Premises Development Plan and prioritised accordingly
- Check whether any surveys are due for revision, e.g. condition survey, asbestos survey, fire safety audit
- Review and update the Premises Development Plan with the SAFE Committee
- Inventory/Asset Register check – one of the governors attends to carry out a 'spot check' on the inventory and report to the SAFE Committee regarding this
- Equipment leases and contracts – review these to ensure they are suitable for the school's needs
- Review DRBCP and run through scenarios to ensure it is still effective

Professional development

Knowledge gained during my School Business Management Certificate training was valuable as one of the modules was premises management. I am now part way through the Diploma of School Business Management and this is helping me to think on a more strategic level and as a result I feel I am making a more valuable contribution to the development of the premises.

My knowledge has also developed through reading and research as well as working collaboratively with colleagues and tapping into the expertise of skilled colleagues via various forums.

I have attended a number of health and safety training courses covering areas such as risk assessments, fire safety, contractor management and general health and safety. These courses were very useful and the documentation received is a good source of information to refer back to if needed.

Performance management of staff is used to identify any gaps in skills to enable a focused training programme to support staff development. Staff development is a worthwhile investment and I ensure that the relevant staff have received training in the areas of health and safety training, fire, COSHH, legionella and asbestos, etc. I maintain a training record to track when refresher training is required.

The future

The future holds more challenges for the SBM; with decreases in funding predicted school budgets will be tighter, highlighting the need to obtain value for money across all aspects of the budget. One of the rewarding aspects of the role, and one which will increase in importance, is to be involved in the whole school strategic planning, to think creatively about income generation and innovative use of the school premises so that our focus on educational improvement can be maintained effectively.

6e. Case Study – A Secondary Perspective

Martin Shevill Principal of Ossett Academy and Sixth Form College Wakefield describes how his school managed a major building project.

Context

Ossett Academy is an 11-18 co-education non-selective academy with over 1800 students, approximately 450 of whom are in the sixth form. There are six types of architecture on the site including an old Victorian house, a 1930's grammar school building, extensive clasp construction buildings from 1970, a 1980's block and two large modern buildings erected this century. We also possess six temporary classrooms. The site is relatively compact for 1800+ students and playing fields are a third of a mile away. Our challenges relate to the maintenance of a very full building that receives a great deal of wear and tear and has a variety of old building stock. The academy is also built on a slope which adds to the complexity. The site would never be chosen for a new build and the original school on this site had less than 100 students.

Refurbishment project – Vision and redesign

The key driver for refurbishment was to improve curriculum teaching spaces in part of our 1980's building particularly for English, which we felt required a designated space close to the Maths area located in an adjacent newer block, to achieve some parity of accommodation.

The English department had been housed in scattered accommodation with four temporary classrooms. The ground floor included five classrooms, a small teaching space and a girls' toilet. The first floor of this building included five classrooms, a large store room and a boys' toilet. The space was part of the humanities area, tired looking and used inefficiently.

The vision was to create more collaboration between the core subjects of English and Maths and give them a joint status as lead subjects.

A key element to the refurbishment was the redesign of the first floor. Three of the classrooms and the large store space have been converted into two large teaching spaces. These rooms are now used for double groups of students in Maths or English with two teachers and a learning mentor. This enables more effective differentiated group work along with the pairing of an experienced teacher with a relatively new teacher.

The emphasis has been to drive more imaginative teaching styles and create more flexible setting structures. All the other teaching spaces in this block have been refurbished with new flooring, doors, lighting and decoration. Wall displays have been removed and each room now has one large piece of contemporary art work. The two large teaching spaces are separated from the corridor space by large glass partitions. The toilet areas are now break-out rooms with computers. (A new toilet block had been completed prior to this project in a central area of the academy site).

The successful translation of vision into reality is best demonstrated by the fact that the new joint area is affectionately referred to as the 'Manglish' area.

Role of governors

Two committees were involved. The Curriculum Committee were keen to see an improvement in the learning environment of Maths and English. The project reflected ambitious changes we wanted to introduce to the academy in terms of our 'Learning Revolution'. This is a whole school initiative to raise student engagement and create more active learning. Creating the right environment was part of the vision.

The Resources Committee were fully involved in each stage of the development and this clearly linked to the vision from the Curriculum Committee. Spending was approved and governors were keen to be involved in discussing the anticipated outcomes to changes in pedagogy, setting practices and the environment for learning.

The project was funded internally. Grants were acquired for other projects for replacement windows, asbestos removal and new piping and this freed up monies for our own re-design project. Our best value considerations were based on improving results in Maths and English and creating a more professional and business-like environment for our students. This was successfully achieved!

The role of the School Business Manager

Much of the work both pre and during refurbishment fell onto our SBM who project managed the initiative from inception to completion, including painting walls on the Sunday before the start of the autumn term!

The SBM was supported by our Premises Development Manager who led his team of staff (all employees of the academy) in almost all the refurbishment activities. A small number of specialists were brought in at key times. Using our own skilled staff meant that the impact on the day-to-day work of the academy was minimal.

Work started in earnest in the last two weeks of summer term of 2012. The Humanities team had to be re-housed during this period and substitute rooms were used for timetabled teaching. The internal modification and room refurbishments part of the project were completed during the six weeks of the summer holiday. We did however underestimate the time required to undertake some of the IT work, such as cabling, installing new network points and introducing 'Apple TV' into this area.

The process was monitored throughout by the SBM. Senior staff frequently checked the progress over the summer holiday. The real success factor of this project was that it was almost entirely completed 'in-house' with materials procured by our premises team.

We were fortunate in that we were able to rely very heavily on our own staff's goodwill and excellent team ethos to work weekends and evenings, to ensure the building was ready for use at the start of the term. With hindsight, the IT infrastructure should have been scheduled earlier.

We ordered a large number of trapezoid tables, with a view to them forming large octagon shapes with a space in the middle. When they arrived we found that the size and shape did not fit our space as planned so we improvised and made horseshoes shape instead. These actually work much better for learning as large groups can be spilt into smaller groups with a teacher or learning mentor in the centre of each horseshoe, working with the students.

Evaluation of impact

Results at GCSE have improved massively. This is a result of better differentiated teaching in more appropriate and attractive spaces and there has been a 'wow factor'. The spaces are unrecognisable. Students and staff really do feel invested in.

Success factors

Effective budget planning and involvement of the governing body committees to monitor this

- The project was also clearly linked to the teaching objectives of our development plan (Ossett's learning revolution) and again approved by governors
- The Student Council had also been consulted about learning environments and stated that they would appreciate brighter, more attractive learning spaces
- Conscious decisions to spend more money on certain elements, for example the quality of the flooring and additional computers to source better quality materials which can be a saving in the longer term
- All materials and furnishing were carefully costed

Outcomes have clearly been positive and this is the type of project we would repeat if we ever find the correct spaces within the academy and are able to identify funding. In future we would budget for higher project costs.

6f. Top Tips for Premises and Facilities Management – Including Additions to the SBM's Job Description

1. Refer to Section 3.5 of our Effective Governance guide for more information about the premises related responsibility of governors and the link with the Ofsted framework
2. Refer to Section 3.5 of our Effective Governance guide for a case study identifying the role of governors in developing the physical resources of the school
3. Draw up a Premises Development Plan, using an external consultant if needs be. This will underpin any developments and capital bids you may want to make. It will ensure you are ready to develop bids when the need arises. Make sure this plan is based upon anticipated pupil numbers and the school vision
4. Carry out annual Condition Surveys to ensure buildings are safe and to prioritise repair and maintenance work in a cost-effective way
5. Have an annual repair and refurbishment programme no matter how modest. It shows the school and community you care about the fabric
6. Ensure that there is a clear line of accountability to the relevant Governors Committee and co-opt the Site Manager or Caretaker onto the Committee. This will work wonders for their self-esteem and ownership of tasks
7. Ensure that there is a clear system for reporting health and safety Issues so that they can be addressed
8. Ensure that good records are kept on risk assessments, legionella tests, PAT tests, the asbestos register, fire safety (including test fire drills) etc
9. Don't be afraid to find your own architect rather than being tied in to the Local Authority
10. Make sure faults are put right quickly – damage, graffiti etc proliferates if it is seen as normal
11. Monitor the work of contractors, even if you are a Local Authority Maintained School. This includes the Grounds Maintenance contractors
12. Review the lettings charges so that they keep pace with costs (lighting, heating, cleaning, caretakers) and that they are not far behind rival facilities

Additions to the SBM's Job Description

It is a common axiom that the School Business Manager's role has expanded exponentially and it is not unusual for the SBM to undertake a range of activities for premises and facilities management.

Be prepared

The following responsibilities might be included in the SBM job description:

- To ensure the school facilities are used to best advantage in terms of maximising income
- To line-manage and oversee the work of the Site Manager and his team, including the cleaning team
- To oversee all appointments to the Premises Team, involving the Site Manager and Cleaning Manager as appropriate
- To performance manage the Site Manager and to ensure appropriate performance management of the site team is undertaken

Underpinning this strategic responsibility for the performance of the site team the SBM would need to work with the Site Manage to establish and maintain effective monitoring and recording systems for:

- Routine risk assessments, health and safety issues, faults and repairs
- Quality and consistency of cleaning and grounds maintenance

There might be specific references to working with senior leaders and governors, for example:

- To attend governing body meetings related to premises matters and advise on strategic and operational projects including the Condition Survey and proposed works for the ensuing year
- To ensure governors are aware of their health and safety responsibilities and to provide information to support them
- With the Headteacher ensure policies, systems and recording procedures are reviewed and fit for purpose
- To ensure that accurate and timely information is considered by the Headteacher and Senior Leadership Team to enable them to plan premises development. This will include offering advice on premises budget levels, and the potential impact on other staffing and curriculum budgets

The role of the SBM to support building projects might also be identified:

- To commission contractors when required. To deal with specifications for work to be carried out and the process of deciding on which contractor is appointed in line with the Financial Procedures Manual
- To draw up bids for Capital Funds such as the Academies Capital Maintenance Fund (ACMF) and work with the architect as appropriate
- To work with the school's architect to ensure that Building Contractors are working to schedule, that the site set-up is safe, that there is agreement about working practices (i.e. no contact with children, no swearing

  or

- With the Site Manager to oversee the quality and timeliness of work undertaken by contractors
- To oversee the management of dual use facilities for example a Sports Hall

Throughout this guide our case studies recognise the important strategic role the SBM plays in budget planning, ensuring support for school priorities and the positive impact on school improvement. Strategic responsibility for premises and facilities is another important facet of the role.

Chapter 7

Bid Writing Including Capital Funding Grants

7a. Introduction

This chapter looks at the role of the School Business Manager in writing and submitting a successful bid to the EFA for a capital grant.

Focus of the chapter

This chapter will identify some important elements of a successful bid and give the SBM confidence in their approach to compiling the appropriate documentation.

The key questions a SBM should think about and governors should ask are:

- How does the project relate to the school asset management plan, risk register and EFA key areas for funding?
- What initial planning, for example applying for planning consent, can be done to facilitate a speedy start to the project if the bid is successful?
- Have any costs relating to this initial planning been identified?
- What are the projected costs and are they spread over more than one year?
- Are there risks to spreading the cost in this way?
- How will the project be managed if successful?
- How confident are we that the project will be completed on time and in budget?
- What is the potential impact on the day-to-day running of the school?
- What are the expected outcomes of the project in terms of school improvement?

Context

All schools have Devolved Formula Capital, which is not sufficient for major projects but does support cyclical maintenance and some minor refurbishments.

Maintained schools have to rely on the Local Authority to provide money for capital projects usually linked to urgent health and safety needs. The Local Authority ranks these projects according to their own condition survey in order of need, before allocating any money and will then discuss with the school how much they will be expected to contribute. The process is not always seen as objective and can mean that the devolved capital formula has to be allocated to the project for one or more years thus putting at risk the opportunity to redecorate or refurbish other parts of the building.

There is also Targeted Basic Needs Funding for expanding schools and new schools where there are insufficient places. In this case the Local Authority puts in the bids and these have to be approved by the Education Funding Agency (EFA).

The EFA currently allocates funding for maintenance and expansions to academies through the Academies Capital Maintenance Fund (ACMF) and operates a bidding process, which is more transparent and objective in operation.

The ACMF application process has been designed to be short and simple. Academies need to complete a single page form per project to make their case for funding. The EFA advises academies to draw on information that they already have, such as building condition survey data, as evidence for their building needs. Less information is expected for smaller or simpler projects to minimise unnecessary bureaucracy. The EFA expects that academies with larger or more complex projects to be able to briefly, but adequately, demonstrate that they or their consultants have the appropriate skills and resources to deliver them.

For more information about ACMF go to www.gov.uk/efa

The opportunity to bid for capital grants from the EFA's Academy Capital Maintenance Fund is an attraction when schools are considering a change of status to academy.

The ACMF is currently the main vehicle for academies to access funding for building condition needs, but this may change in the future. By improving the quality and consistency of condition data across the education estate the DfE aims to develop a more structured maintenance programme for all schools. The EFA is delivering this by carrying out the Property Data Survey Programme, the most comprehensive survey of the condition of school buildings ever carried out, which was published in March 2014. For more information go to www.gov.uk/government/publications/property-data-survey-programme

Whatever the future of maintenance funding for academies, it is likely that there will be on-going opportunities for academies to bid for funds from the EFA, as well as other organisations such as Sport England. It is important that SBMs are aware of these opportunities and are able to make clear and concise bids.

We have asked the EFA for tips on what makes a good capital bid, based on their experience of running ACMF and other major bid rounds. Other case studies explain how they prepared a successful bid and the impact on their school.

7b. Successful Bid Writing for a Capital Grant

The Education Funding Agency explains the importance of thorough preparation

1. Read the bid guidance

The guidance for the bid round will usually include pointers on what the assessors are looking for and some hints and tips on putting forward your bid. Those who are assessing the bids are interested in receiving clear bids that are targeted at the criteria, so they will be happy to clarify anything that is not clear. The bid guidance will also set out who is eligible to bid and how bids should be returned.

It is important to plan out the process of preparing your bid to ensure you allow sufficient time for review and checking before the bid deadline. The EFA often sees a last minute surge in applications being sent in on the deadline day.

2. Establish the need

In the latest round of Academies Capital Maintenance Fund (ACMF) half of the marks available to applications allocated were allocated to the following criteria:

> "EITHER
>
> (for building condition related projects) the urgency / importance of the building condition issues being tackled through the project and/or benefits for the school from the investment
>
> OR
>
> (for expansion projects) the number of new places being added at successful schools and/or the urgency of dealing with overcrowding given demand for places"

This sends a clear message that the first and most important part of any bid is establishing the need for investment at your academy. This is likely to be the case for other bidding rounds as well. Establishing a clear need for a project starts with having good asset management information available to you so that you can clearly prioritise the need within your own buildings. The EFA allocates most ACMF funds for building condition issues. An up-to-date condition survey will highlight the urgency of addressing building issues across the site and help you to build your case for funding. The EFA will prioritise the replacement of items that have actually failed, or are highly likely to fail where you can provide evidence from a suitable professional that a repair is not possible and/or more expensive than a replacement.

The large majority of bid rounds are over-subscribed, so it is also important to show the urgency of the work and why this is not a proposal that could be deferred to be considered again at a future round. That isn't to say that projects that aren't urgent can't be successful, but they would then need to demonstrate excellent value for money and show a low delivery risk.

Where you are increasing places or for example increasing the size of a kitchen, it is a good idea to include some relevant research you have undertaken to support your bid such as questionnaires to parents. It can also improve your chances of success if the school will allocate some money towards the cost.

3. Develop a clear solution

You will need to demonstrate that projects have been well thought through, repairs have been considered rather than simple replacement and risks considered appropriately. A thorough option appraisal (including a do nothing option) will help build the case for your proposed project.

Knowing what your project is and being able to convey your requirements clearly and concisely is essential. The EFA believes that if an academy is having trouble and going way over the word count on the form, it may well be that they need to develop a clearer project plan. In some cases it might actually be more than one project. It is worth bearing in mind that evidence that a project is vital to the operation of the school, has been thought through appropriately and is ready to deliver will be ranked higher.

4. Ensure the solution is deliverable

You should also consider what risks there are to delivering the project. Discovering additional asbestos once work has begun is the most common reason for delay or cost over-runs to ACMF projects — once the EFA has made an allocation, they can only increase it in exceptional circumstances. An up-to-date survey will help you to understand the risks and your responsibilities around asbestos and gives potential contractors a useful reference point when they are providing a quote for works.

For larger schemes most academies will need to draw on technical advisers to:

- develop the design
- secure planning approval
- oversee procurement and manage the project

For managing smaller schemes in-house, you may wish to get advice about specifications of particular products so you don't waste money-buying items, such as windows etc., which will fail in five years' time.

If you would need to manage work being done on site during term time, you need to understand the key issues and risks that will need to be managed, particularly if the works require more than one contractor on site at one time. Consider as far as possible whether there are ways to avoid expenditure on temporary accommodation, as this will erode the value for money case for the project. Build in a figure for contingency which will help address many of the issues.

5. Value for money

You should consider obtaining a quote for the works prior to submitting a bid. Consider also the ability of the school team to project manage; it may be more cost effective to employ someone from the beginning of the feasibility process if the bid is critical to your needs.

This helps build confidence in the costs you are presenting and indicates that the project is close to being ready to go. Academies are responsible for procuring works and ensuring that good value is secured for the public purse. The EFA will be assessing your scheme against similar schemes from other academies, so it is important to ensure that you are paying an appropriate market rate for the works. On larger schemes, a technical adviser should be able to advise you of a reasonable price for the project.

7c. The Secondary Experience

Alison Wyatt, Bursar, the Midsomer Norton Schools Partnership – a Hard Federation of two secondary schools in Midsomer Norton

We have been successful with several bids to the Academies Capital Maintenance Fund (ACMF). Two of these, when complete, will have replaced all of the temporary buildings on the Norton Hill School site. This was our top priority and, fortunately, it was also one of the EFA key areas for funding. We had been trying for many years to persuade the Local Authority to replace these classrooms without success, despite the fact that they had been identified as in urgent need of replacement on the LA's own Building Condition Survey.

Other successful bids have been for window replacements, roof repairs, boiler and toilet replacements. These were not necessarily a top priority but as they matched the EFA's key areas for funding, we bid for them anyway. Obviously, the fact that we have been able to attract this capital funding has meant we have not had to spend our money on these areas which has allowed us to use it for other things.

The bidding process does not allow for reams of information to be submitted, so it is essential that the best use is made of the limited amount of space for narrative and evidence to support the bid.

In my opinion key areas to focus on are:

- Demonstrate the need and quote the evidence to support it (eg Building Condition Survey). Health and safety issues help to justify the need and these can be amplified if necessary!
- Demonstrate how the project will lead to improved outcomes for pupils
- Include information on floor area and costs, ensuring this fits within EFA guidelines for costs per metre
- Include information on the number of pupils and classrooms that the project will have an impact on
- Demonstrate value for money. For example, what will be saved in terms of on-going repair and maintenance costs currently being expended in order to keep the existing facilities running? What will be saved in terms of energy costs because the changes are more energy efficient?
- Demonstrate how the project will be achieved within the EFA funding cycle. In one case, we split the original project into two separate projects, bidding for the second project one year after the first. This meant that the projects could be delivered individually within much shorter timescales. This would not at first glance appear to be the best way forward as clearly there would have been economies of scale to be gained by building the project as a whole. It's a question of getting the best match for the EFA criteria
- Demonstrate how the project will be managed. Will there be a bought-in Project Manager? Also demonstrate that the school is able to manage the project during term time, and how. A school team with experience of this helps
- Demonstrate that as much as possible has been done up front. This will incur some

cost to the school and demonstrates commitment. This will range from asbestos testing to preparation of a full planning application by a professional architect

- If possible, commit some of your own funds to the project. This helps to ensure value for money for the EFA and demonstrates the school's commitment

To back up the bid it is possible to submit up to eight pages in a zipped up folder of no more than 3MB. Documents I would recommend including are:

- Photographs showing the existing facility in the worst possible light, eg mould, damp, condensation, leaks. Take photographs on a dismal bleak day, not when the sun is shining!
- Extracts from independent reports such as the Local Authority's Building Condition Survey, or any of your own reports such as your own Condition Survey, the asbestos register etc. which demonstrate the poor condition of existing facilities
- Architect drawings for the new facility
- The likely costs of the project. This could range from a simple quotation for a smaller project to a full Quantity Surveyor costing for a large project
- A Gantt chart showing the project timescale with key milestones
- A chart showing cash-flow, demonstrating how the EFA funds will be spent to their timescale

Once the bids were successful my role was:

- To follow the correct purchasing procedures, which for larger projects will include going out to tender. This is a service which could also be handled by a professional project manager
- To ensure the projects were completed to timescale and within budget
- To manage contractors working on site during term time, ensuring normal school operations and health and safety standards were maintained
- To facilitate discussions between contractors and interested parties, for example the school's ICT team, to ensure needs were being correctly met
- To organise the fitting out of new rooms with furniture, blinds etc
- To ensure snagging items addressed within warranty period

I have found the success in bidding for Capital Funds to be very rewarding, both for me personally and for the academies. I felt a huge sense of achievement when we were able finally to see the back of forty year-old temporary classrooms after continually failing to persuade the Local Authority to address this issue!

7d. Top Tips for Successful Capital Bids

1. Refer to Section 1 of our Effective Governance guide which explains the role of governors in determining the strategic direction of the school
2. Refer to Section 3.5 of our Effective Governance guide for more information about the premises related responsibility of governors
3. Ensure the school has a comprehensive and up to date condition survey which identifies urgent health and safety work
4. Link these needs to school improvement priorities and potential impact on pupil outcomes
5. Read the EFA guidance carefully and target your application
6. Prepare well ahead, for example with surveys including that for asbestos, photographs, architect's drawings, indicative costs and planning consent if necessary
7. Ensure your bid is realistic: consider replacement or repair rather than new build
8. Ensure governors are supportive of the bid and prepared to budget for any preparation costs or relevant subsequent work undertaken at school expense
9. Build a contingency figure into the budget
10. Develop a clear project plan and be concise but focused when filling in the form
11. Plan the work so that the project can be completed within the time frame set by the EFA
12. Demonstrate value for money and the importance of the project to the strategic development of the school and pupil outcomes

Chapter 8

Income Generation

8a. Introduction

This chapter looks at the role of the School Business Manager in helping the school generate income.

Focus of the chapter

This chapter is intended to give the School Business Manager some confidence in how to go about generating extra income for their school.

Key questions

- Who has oversight of income generation in the school?
- Is this part of the strategic plan or is it an add-on, with little or no coherent or determined effort?
- What role do the governors play, if any?
- How do parents and other members of the community contribute?
- What use does the school make of its facilities to raise funds?
- What use does the school make of other assets and resources?
- Does income generation get reported to the Governors Finance Committee?
- What have been the school's successes in generating income?
- How does this compare to other schools?

Context

Increasingly schools are looking to generate additional income to supplement funding from the Government. As Schools Minister, Lord Nash, said at The Academies Show in April 2014:

> "One thing nobody should be under any illusion about is that is whichever government is in power there is going to be a shortage of money for schools in the foreseeable future. Schools should plan for flat line revenues which, bearing in mind that schools are having to do so much more, means they have to start thinking out of the box in terms of their financial management."

Clearly, income generation is going to become increasingly important to make up shortfalls in revenue.

Too often, schools only think of school lettings as a source of income. Utilising school facilities, when they are not in use for teaching purposes, not only raises funds but also can contribute to community development and demonstrates effective use of public resources. It is also a way of marketing the school as the public crosses the threshold and is impressed by what they see!

Of course, just letting out the school facilities is one way of raising funds from the school's physical resources; there are many other approaches to this.

It pays to be proactive about utilising school facilities for income generation. Marketing what you have, thinking of less obvious ways for the public to use your facilities is important. For example, one school has spotted the demand for spaces for children's parties and now raises significant funds as a children's party organiser. This brings in their catering team and their facilities too.

An extension of the lettings programme could be running activities after school or during the school holidays. The Extended Schools Programme signposted this, but many ventures fell away when funding was withdrawn. Of course, many primary schools will run after-school or pre-school activities. These may or may not have income generation as a motive, but the opportunity is there.

Similarly, the need for children's activities during the school holidays, especially the long summer break, can be seen as an opportunity to generate income.

Other income generating activities will be down to the individual circumstances of the school. You need to think about the types of assets and resources that your school possesses and which could be used to generate income.

An example of this might be the knowledge and expertise of your staff. You may have staff who are expert in specific areas of the curriculum or school management (or any aspect of education for that matter). They may be able to run courses on a commercial basis or be hired by other schools to deliver INSET. They might develop curriculum materials which could be published and sold. Innovative Schemes of Work, resources, assessment packages, training materials are all resources which other schools may be interested in purchasing.

One secondary school raised huge amounts of income through developing an ICT course, which it then sold to other schools along with a support and training package.

Of course, one obvious asset is the school community itself. There are examples of schemes whereby internet purchases can raise funds for schools. If parents, staff and supporters of a school join an internet site such as easyfundraising.org.uk then every purchases made by clicking through their site can achieve a donation of between 1% and 3% of the amount spent. With the increases in internet shopping this could be an easy way for a school to generate income.

How do you go about developing an income generation strategy?

There are four basic steps here:

1. Identify your assets
   a. school facilities – buildings and grounds
   b. school resources and equipment catering, computers, technology etc
   c. staff knowledge and expertise

2. Assess the opportunities to generate income from your school's assets
3. If your assessment is viable:
   a. develop the idea so it can be marketed
   b. put in place consistent and robust procedures to manage the activity
4. Have timelines so that you take stock and evaluate the income generating activity and closedown if necessary

In doing this you must always try to ensure you know the true cost of the activity and include:

- Wear and tear
- Depreciation of assets (such as computers)
- Heating, lighting, cleaning
- Staff costs in administration and site staff etc

You must also balance any risks (i.e. is it prudent and safe to rent out your vacant computer room to a local organisation during school hours?) against the potential benefits.

Income generation may also be best achieved by partnering with other schools to increase the scope of income generation opportunities. It may also be an activity which will benefit from some dedicated staff time. Some schools have appointed Income Generation Managers (or Business Development Managers). Sometimes this has simply been a paid post, at other times the appointed person has had a salary supplemented by performance related pay based on the amount of income generated. Yet other schools have only paid the Development Manager a proportion of the income raised – thus minimizing the risk of paying a salary and not raising income!

Finally, in all of this, you need to make sure that an income generation activity is not detrimental to your pupils' educational experience.

As Lord Nash indicated, there is likely to be a shortage of central funding for schools in the foreseeable future and, against this backdrop, schools will have to get more creative in respect of income generation. Schools have a variety of resources at their disposal which can be used to raise income:

- Trading services
- Knowledge capital
- Physical assets

With an imaginative, entrepreneurial approach these can be utilised to raise surprisingly large revenues.

Whilst some schools may be reluctant to involve themselves in commercial activities, seeing this as a move away from a pure focus on education, the question is, in the modern climate, is this an affordable stance?

8b. The Secondary Experience

Martin Kerslake, Director of Finance and Business Services at Priory Community School, Weston-Super-Mare, explains how he set up a trading company and the impact on revenue.

First steps

We wanted to establish a vehicle that the Academy could use to develop a range of services with the sole aim of providing additional income streams to support the work of the Academy.

We set up Priory Community School Enterprises Limited (PCSE) which was incorporated under the Companies Act 2006 as a private company on the 8th August 2011. PCSE is wholly owned by Priory Community School an Academy Trust. A master agreement between the Academy and PCSE was created to ensure that the legal relationship was clearly defined.

The company

The formation of the private company and its structure enables any profit to be gift-aided at the end of each trading year to the Academy. This ensures that no corporation tax liability arises.

The governors were an integral part of the decision making. We have always been mindful of being able to develop other income streams that would be of benefit to the Academy in the future. The formation of PCSE enabled the provision of a vehicle for this to be a reality. Not having a separate company would have meant that we would be restricted to the terms of the Articles of Association of the Academy which only related to educational and community activities.

We felt that governors should be able to control the company and thus three governors and two officers were appointed as directors. The initial directors appointed comprised of the Chair of Governors, the Chair of the Business and Site Committee, a further governor from the Business and Site Committee, the Director of Finance and Business Services and the Manager of the health and safety traded service. These five directors form the Board of the company.

Tax and VAT

There were a number of key decisions which we made to facilitate the incorporation of the company. From the financial compliance perspective we needed to consider the position with regard to tax and VAT.

With regard to VAT we entered into a group registration, which was one of the first, if not the first in the country, for such an arrangement for an academy.

The trading company has a separate bank account which is audited at the same time as the academy accounts. We work with our accountants throughout the year to identify and mitigate our tax liability as effectively as possible.

Operational management

The day-to-day operations of PCSE are the responsibility of the Director of Finance and Traded Services. Currently a number of traded services are provided by the company, including a traded health and safety service, a lettings service and a traded teaching and learning service.

The Academy utilises Capita SIMS Financial Management System (FMS) for recording its financial transactions and it has a separate FMS licence under which it records all transactions to do with the trading company

The Board of PCSE meets termly to review the activities being undertaken and to receive reports. The financial progress of PCSE is part of the financial reporting undertaken termly to the Governors' Business and Site Committee. The end of year trading results are fed into the main academy accounts which are presented to the Full Governing Body.

Income Generation

PCSE was established in August 2011. The following table shows the amounts gift-aided to the Academy:

Financial year ending	Amount
31/8/2012	£44,873
31/8/2013	£102,951

The hard work in setting up the company, the bank accounts, and the financial mechanisms has been worth it. We have efficient systems in place which will enable us to add to the portfolio of traded services and other operations and we are thus in a strong position to grow the business and attract additional income into the Academy.

The ethos of the Academy is to do the very best for the students and we believe that exploring a variety of other income streams is important to ensure that we can continue to deliver the best possible education opportunities for our students. In a world of ever decreasing income from the EFA this is an important consideration for all academies.

8c. Examples of Income Generation

There are many ways for schools to generate income. Two primary schools told us their tale.

Lorraine Knight, School Business Manager, Baschurch CE Primary School, Shrewsbury:
"In a rural village with a secondary school, an FE College and a village hall, our opportunities for lettings were minimal. By offering lettings at a slightly reduced price we now have lettings five nights a week. As a result, although we have kept charges to a minimum we will generate £5000 this year after costs".

Lynn Marshall, Bursar, Hartwell Primary School, Northamptonshire:
"We decided to explore the installation of solar panels. The opportunity arose for the school to install solar energy and the governors agreed that it was good use of available monies. The initial outlay was £22,650. This generated £6,976 over 24 months to offset against rising energy costs".

FASNA Members have listed many other basic ideas which may be of interest such as:

- Two schools agreed to send one of their caretakers on an accredited course to do professional electrical checks. The costs of the course and the test equipment, were less than a thousand pounds. The annual savings for the school were high as they could then test their own equipment and also provide this service, at a competitive rate to other local schools
- One school had a member of the Support Staff Team trained to do health and safety checks on work placements. This service was hired out to other schools
- Making an agreement with Exam Revision Company who take over the entire school at holiday time to run their courses
- Hiring out sports fields to organisations that run soccer schools and summer camps
- Using the school for car parking at times when there is demand – examples include schools near sports venues when parking is at a premium; during local festivals or carnivals etc
- Putting commercial links onto the school's website. One school received a water-cooler and lifetime supply of water for putting a link to the company's website on the school's website at no cost to the school
- Working with universities and colleges to support teacher training by contributing to their professional studies programme, delivering lectures and seminars, providing observation and other elements of ITT
- Running courses for other schools. Examples here include:
    - Curriculum design – such as the Thomas Telford ICT courses
    - Child protection courses (needed for all staff at regular intervals)
    - Managing behaviour
    - Special needs (aspergers; autism etc)
    - Educational management etc
    - Support staff development
- Schools have sold specific back office services such as:
    - ICT support
    - ICT repairs

- Payroll
- CRB checks
- Financial support
- Printing and photocopying
- Website design
- Schools have sold specific educational services such as:
  - Music or language specialists hired out
  - Science technician support
  - Specialist sports teaching and coaching
  - Outdoor pursuits
- Schools have used their kitchens for meals on wheels and to provide meals for other schools. An unusual example here is one school making all the sandwiches and filled rolls for another school
- A local church whose congregation has outgrown its own church building uses one school for all its Sunday services
- Having local sports teams use the schools pitches as their home ground
- Some schools report buying in bulk and selling on at a profit
- Hiring out the schools facilities for commercial training
- Having local companies sponsor the school's sports teams and their kit and equipment

Fosse Way School

David Gregory, Headteacher of Fosse Way Special School in Midsomer Norton near Bath, describes how his school went on to establish its own Café Gallery as an educational experience and training facility for older pupils.

Fosse Way School is a special school for 190 pupils aged 3–19 years old. It takes pupils from a wide geographical area including several different Local Authorities (currently five different LAs). In 2011 Fosse Way became an Academy. It is also a Teaching School and is graded 'Outstanding' by Ofsted.

Fosse Way School Café Gallery

Cafe Gallery is on-site beside the school reception area and is modelled upon a high street coffee outlet. It provides:

- A meeting place for parents (important to our parents as they can feel isolated within the community), visiting professionals and local residents
- A genuine business where students help to prepare food, serve customers and discover what is involved in running a business thereby learning and developing, through practical experience, valuable skills that increase their employability on leaving school
- An opportunity to draw in the local community and challenge stereotypical views about disability

The café provides an exhibition space to demonstrate the creativity of students through art and craft exhibitions, and an outlet for produce from the school gardens.

Our learners were involved at all stages of the café development including product design for the menu, customer research and coming up with the name!

Cafe Gallery is a relaxed meeting place, open to all: local community, parents, carers, friends and families. There is free internet access. Cafe Gallery highlights local food producers and forges links with local businesses.

As a teaching school Fosse Way provides a range of training events for the staff of schools across the local area. The café provides the catering for these events as well as other off-site events.

The café manager previously managed a restaurant in the city of Bath and hence brings.a commercial approach to the business. The manager employs an assistant in addition to specially trained school staff who provide 'low profile' support to students. The business looks to be non-profit making with the goal of breaking even. As the principle purpose of the 'business' is education VAT is not payable.

8d. Setting up a Trading Company

Hannah Kubie a senior associate with Stone King solicitors explains how to set up a Trading Company.

As academies continue to expand and become more business-like, it is inevitable that some of their activities will go beyond only teaching and learning within the academy. A number of academies now also provide childcare facilities, leisure facilities, specialist advice courses, collaborate with other schools, or set up facilities or activities for their students.

Academies are therefore now increasingly looking to set up a trading company in order to enable them to grow in terms of their size and activities.

Why would an academy trust set up a trading company?

Permitted activities – An Academy Trust, as a type of charity, should not carry out activities which are outside of its purposes. All Academy Trusts are set up to 'advance education' and some have other additional objects (such as to promote recreational leisure and to operate a children's centre). An Academy Trust may not set up a trading company for any reason, but may do so to advance its purposes or to fundraise. A trading company can generally carry out a wider range of activities compared to an Academy Trust, if it is for fundraising purposes.

Further, activities other than running education at the academy cannot usually benefit from General Annual Grant.

Ring- fencing risk – As some trading activities carry inherent risks, the Academy Trust should consider protection in the form of ring-fencing risky trading activities. Even if an Academy Trust has purposes which include promoting recreational leisure, for instance, it may choose to operate a leisure centre through a trading subsidiary, particularly where risks are involved.

Tax – If the trading company transfers any profit it generates from its trading activities up to the Academy Trust, this can be done so in a tax efficient way because such charitable donations reduce the trading company's corporation tax liability. If it donates all its taxable profits to the Academy Trust, the trading company will pay no corporation tax at all.

Procurement – Although beyond the scope of this article, if an Academy Trust (or several) set up a wholly owned subsidiary, if structured properly, the Academy Trust may treat provision of services by the trading company to the Academy Trust as 'in-house' and outside the scope of the public procurement rules.

Relationship between the Academy Trust and the trading company

As a charity, the Academy Trust is required to deal with the trading company at 'arm's length'. For example, crucially, there must be no mixing of funds. We would also recommend that at least one or two Directors (two is better practice) of the trading company are independent from the Academy Trust so that conflicts can be managed between the two organisations. Although these conflicts might feel academic as the Academy Trust owns/controls the trading company, such independence is good practice and follows Charity Commission guidance.

It is common practice for a simple contract to be put in place between the two entities to ensure their dealings with each other are satisfactory.

Funding – Initial funding of the trading company by the Academy Trust should take the form of a market-rate loan, possibly with security being taken.

Premises/assets – If the trading company is to operate from the Academy Trust's site, this should be documented under an agreement which apportions costs between the two entities.

Management of the trading company – Essentially, the most important factor for the Academy Trust is understanding the independence arrangements and retaining oversight of what the trading company is doing. As such, written records will need to be kept to show all dealings, and to demonstrate that dealings are on an 'arm's length' basis.

How to set up a trading company

Stage 1 – The Board of Trustees of the Academy Trust should resolve to establish a trading company, subject to having an appropriate business plan. They may wish to resolve to delegate powers to proceed with the company to a committee.

Stage 2 – The committee will be responsible for establishing the trading company, which will be a private company limited by shares (unlike the Academy Trust itself which is a company without a share capital). The Academy Trust will however need to subscribe for shares in the trading company. The committee needs to decide upon initial Directors for the trading company, open a bank account, and make recommendations to the main Board of Trustees as to funding and overall management.

Stage 3 – The Board of Trustees will need to pass a resolution regarding the initial funding of the trading company. It will be necessary to ensure that any funding is a 'qualifying investment' for tax purposes.

Decision time!

As mentioned above, there are a number of factors to consider in deciding whether or not to establish a trading company. Often it is essential for an Academy Trust to set up a trading company, for example, if it wants to carry out an activity which is beyond their core purpose but from which it will make a profit. However, sometimes it is a conscious decision to reduce risk or expand the school's activities which leads to setting up a trading company.

If you think that setting up a trading company is the right move for your academy, dependent on the timings of meetings and the preparation of a business plan, the Academy Trust could have one set up in as little as 3 weeks.

Should you require any further advice on setting up a trading company, please do not hesitate to contact Hannah Kubie of Stone King LLP: hannahkubie@stoneking.co.uk or 020 7324 1756.

8e. Top Tips for Income Generation

1.	Refer to Section 2 of our Effective Governance guide which relates to the responsibility of governors to support and challenge the school and Section 3.4 which relates to the responsibility of governors for financial probity
2.	Have a clear strategy for income generation by:
	a.	Identifying your school's assets including:
		1.	school premises – buildings and grounds
		2.	school resources and equipment catering, computers, technology and catering facilities etc.
		3.	staff knowledge and expertise
	b.	Assessing the opportunities to generate income from your school's assets
	c.	If your assessment is viable:
		1.	develop the idea so it can be marketed
		2.	put in place consistent and robust procedures to manage the activity
	d.	Have timelines and targets so that you take stock and evaluate the income generating activity and make adjustments or close down if necessary
3.	Ensure you know the true cost of the income generation activity including wear and tear, depreciation of assets (such as computers), heating, lighting, cleaning and staff costs, including costs associated with administration and site staff etc
4.	Explore working with other schools to maximize income generating opportunities
5.	Income generation is not everyone's forte, so seek an appropriate existing member of staff who is prepared to take it on or include in the job description for a new appointment when appropriate
6.	Remember, this is about making a profit!

Chapter 9

Managing School Meals

9a. Introduction

This chapter looks at the role of the School Business Manager in overseeing the provision of school meals

---

Focus of the chapter

This chapter is intended to give the SBM some confidence in how to manage and improve the provision of school meals.

Key questions

- Who has oversight of the provision of school meals?
- What are the lines of oversight and accountability?
- Is the service provided in-house or by contractors?
- Is the service profitable or does it run at a loss?
- What role do the governors play, if any?
- How is the provision of school meals reviewed and improved?
- How do parents and pupils have an input into the quality of school meals?
- Does the school make of its catering facilities to raise funds?
- Are school meals finances reported to the Governors Finance Committee?
- How does your school meals provision compare to other schools?

Context

With the announcement in September 2013, that there would be free school meals for all pupils in Reception and Key Stage 1 from September 2014, there has been a renewed focus on how this service can be provided. For many schools this will pose great challenges as they have neither the facilities nor the expertise in place.

It is vital that schools spend some time reviewing their catering arrangements. This is well described in our case studies. Such a review will need to consider:

- The menus, quality and sourcing of ingredients
- Presentation and food service arrangements
- The suitability and capacity of the dining area
- Price and value for money
- Communication and engagement with parents and pupils in order to encourage take-up

- Opportunities for further improvement and development such as income generation
- On-going communication and review of the service
- The use of pupil and parent surveys both before any substantial changes are implemented and at regular intervals to ensure satisfaction with the service

There will also be the question of whether the service is provided in-house or put out to tender. Whichever route the school opts for there will be the issue of how the service is line-managed. In many schools this falls to the SBM who will either line-manage the catering manager (in-house) or oversee the contractor (outsourced).

The decision over who provides the catering service in the school is one which will need to involve the governors. They will want to look at the alternatives, scrutinize the finances and the specification and be clear about the objectives the school is trying to achieve. What is their vision for the school's catering service? Catering companies charge for the management of the service and the cost of this should be considered against the potential cost and capacity of the school to ensure compliance with regulations, staffing issues and pay roll.

Governors may want a minimalist approach to just meet the national requirements and not make a loss. However, they may take a broader view and want to use the catering service to support the development of social skills and healthy eating habits in pupils, enhance the school ethos and foster a good community relationship by using local suppliers. Whatever their view, it needs to be carefully thought through and articulated before service provision is decided.

The SBM may not have any experience of managing a catering service and will need to seek advice. The Children's Food Trust (CFT) is a good place to start, and there is also the Lead Association for Catering in Education (LACA). The DfE has also set up the Universal Infant Free School Meals (UIFSM) implementation support service to help infant schools and primary schools with an infant's section to deliver the free school meals. This will be a good source of advice and there is the online UIFSM toolkit and the School Food Plan website.

In addition, there are companies that can provide advice on the rules around health and hygiene in kitchens and the regulations about equipment. They can also advise about menus and costs, about training for kitchen staff and help SBMs and kitchen managers network with others.

Our case studies give a variety of different approaches to this issue.

9b. The Primary Experience (1)

Sonia Case, Headteacher of Dulwich Hamlet Junior School in South London describes the journey her school underwent to transform the catering provision.

Context

When I arrived at the school in September 2007, the kitchen and dining room had not been renovated for many years. The traditional pull down kitchen hatch greeted the children who were required to line up (pin themselves against) the wall, squeezing between tables and erratic radiators. The noise in the Victorian hall was awful – not because the children were over-loud, but the combination of chatter, knives and forks, midday supervisors and food serving created an absolute hubbub of unpleasant noise.

The kitchen itself was far too large for what was needed although the actual length of the servery was insufficient. There was the usual pushing and shoving. This, coupled with a dull dinner menu – lumpy mashed potatoes, too many bland dishes and far too frequent diced carrots, meant that lunchtime was the lowlight of each school day. Interestingly the catering contractor was the same as the one we have now.

Initiating Change

It was immediately obvious that the caterers had not been challenged by the leadership team, and had been doing no more than billing us every month and collecting their monies. No-one had looked at whether the contract was delivering value for money, or whether the offering could be improved. We believed that the quality of our catering provision should start with the school vision.

The first thing we did was to set up a working party made up of staff and interested parents. The working party was sometimes challenging with considerable variety of opinion expressed in regard to what parents wanted from a school lunches. For some, health considerations superseded taste or child appeal, whereas for others, they were concerned that their growing child should receive enough bulk to keep them going through the afternoon. Some wanted no desserts other than fresh fruit, others insisted on a range of puddings from sponge to suet!

We were successful in a bid to the Primary Capital Programme and received funding via the Local Authority towards major refurbishments of the dining hall and the kitchen as well as contributing funds of our own. Underfloor heating, acoustic wall tiles, a lowered ceiling, a completely new access to an open plan servery, and new crockery all made the dining experience much more enjoyable: queuing was orderly and conversations were possible.

Out -source or provide in-house?

We considered bringing the catering 'in- house'. We sought the advice of a school down the road doing exactly that and we could see there could be clear benefits. We would be able to source local suppliers particularly a butcher and a greengrocer. We felt that purchasing locally would add real value and endorse our school vision of strong community links.

We then took a long hard look at the risks. In the first year of my Headship, the school underwent a salmonella scare and the catering company was fantastic in managing the many issues that arose: dealing with public health officers, undertaking the numerous health and hygiene inspections, and advising on communication with parents and the wider community. Were the potential very specific health and safety issues which can arise from running your own busy daily kitchen worth taking on, in addition to the overall health and safety issues that arise from daily school life?

Taking on the employment issues of a busy kitchen was something we also had to consider. The need to keep up to date and compliant with training needs and employment issues, cover for sickness, managing irregular shifts and duty rotas would all add to an administrative and organisational burden. We felt that the additional costs could outweigh any potential savings.

Moving forward

We attended procurement training provided by the Local Authority which identified the not inconsiderable responsibilities of procuring and reviewing large contracts. The knowledge that there are a number of catering contractors all keen and 'hungry' for school business means that we are in a much stronger position of negotiation.

We informed our current provider that the contract was under review and invited them to meet with us to consider a way forward. It was only at this point that the real discussions around value for money began in earnest. We had built a good relationship with our school chef who understood the school's needs and vision but was constrained by the way the contract operated.

We renegotiated the contract, moving over time from a rolling contract based on ever changing numbers, to a fixed term contract where there was built-in cost stability and an annual appraisal and renewal.

Re-launching the service

Over a period of time we reached the point where we felt that we could confidently re-launch the meals provision as a new and improved service offering a quality experience to pupils and staff which would have a positive impact on the school learning environment.

A working party of staff, parents and pupils developed a new 'international menu' which caters for the more diverse and sophisticated palate of many of our pupils and which also allows us to include vegetables within the main dish rather than as an adjunct. The menu was key to raising interest amongst our pupils and parents and we went from serving just over 160 dinners a day to our current total of 330 daily lunches.

The retention of the chef was important. Without his culinary skills and abilities to run his kitchen team we would not have transformed our offering.

The company organised some special events for the children; a Year 6 Gala Dinner in which they cooked, alongside the chef, a three course meal for their parents. They learnt culinary and event management skills and it was a lovely way of rounding off their final year.

The Year 5 pupils were given the chance to serve an afternoon cream tea for their parents. And the whole school participated in a Ready Steady Cook event which was a fun interactive way of promoting both cooking and healthy eating.

The future

We will continue to seek excellence from our contract and when we next review we will be considering:

- Quality of food, provenance and recipes
- Working relationship and reactivity to us
- Knowledge and support of employment matters including staff training and welfare
- Value for money
- The added value

We know that there are other companies pitching for school meals provision and we know that many schools successfully run their own service. This makes it all the more important to ensure that the school achieves value for money and that the provision of quality meals in pleasant surroundings is maintained and continues to support the school's vision.

9c. The Primary Experience (2)

Dr Dianne Marshall, Headteacher of Violet Way Primary Academy, Burton-on-Trent, describes how her school has delivered high class provision of school meals.

Context

Eight years ago on becoming a Foundation School we created a vision for catering. Prior to this, as a community school the catering team were working with inflexible menus, poor products and limited support under the direction of County Catering and were becoming increasingly frustrated.

Violet Way Academy is an Outstanding school, and as such prides itself on a significant reputation in the community, high educational standards and commitment to pastoral care. The Governing Body and staff at the school wanted the very best for school meals too. We believed that a transformation in the quality of food provided at mid-day, together with the development of cooking in the curriculum for our young generation, would have a significant impact on their future lives and well-being.

As we engaged on this particular journey, we were very clear about our expectations and ambitions. We started by recognising the child as the customer and asking ourselves "what did we want them to enjoy?" Plastic trays, poor presentation and poor quality of food were no longer options.

We set out to change the quality of food by having fresh fruit and vegetables daily and by using local suppliers wherever possible. We wanted to have salad bowls on the tables and include as daily menu options a vegetarian dish and jacket potatoes with different toppings.

To complement this approach we opted for a more restaurant style atmosphere with table cloths, china crockery and background music.

From vision to reality

In order to realise all of the above, we presented a three-year 'break-even' plan to our governors with realistic costings and anticipated take up revenue which was agreed. The planning, budget projections and careful monitoring were so successful that we broke even within 12 months.

The success necessitated a significant income generation. The initiatives involved in reigning in an 'additional income stream' on a regular basis were not only substantial, but also added a whole new dimension to our school as the centre of its community.

We engaged with the community and the pupils to find out their preferences and menu suggestions as a result of which we have introduced regular 'special cuisine' days. The success generated a significant income stream. Adding to this the catering team has established a 'Celebration Cakes' business making birthday, anniversary and wedding cakes to bespoke order and provides an external catering service to the community and training events at other schools. On Friday afternoon parents are invited in for coffee or tea and have the opportunity to purchase cakes.

Not all successes are measured in £s! Wherever staff are highly valued, given ownership of innovation and consulted regularly morale will grow. Our staff willingly undertook training, completed NVQ qualifications and took themselves to 'sugar craft' evening classes to give the celebration cakes a professional finish. Reception children have the opportunity to have some cookery experience after school and from September 2014 the catering team will offer cookery within curriculum time for the Reception class.

Universal free school meals

With the announcement in September 2013 that all Reception, Year 1 and 2 children would receive a free school meal with effect from September 2014, we felt it was time for an immediate review of our facilities and working patterns!

As an academy we have a 'can do' attitude and, having listened to the announcement on the radio on the way to school, by the time I arrived I had the framework of plan to make this work to our advantage.

We undertook an audit of our current facilities, lunchtime and staffing arrangements. The option of providing a packed lunch would not fit with our philosophy even though without capital improvement of our facilities lunch time would have to extend from 10am to 2pm. Furthermore there would be no time to enable the Celebration Cakes business to continue and the revenue from this helped to support the quality of our meals.

We surveyed parents to get a feel for the potential take up of a hot meal: 99% responded "yes please". We commissioned architects to plan a suitable extension to the kitchen and dining spaces and prepared a bid for capital funding of £90,000. As preparation we began sourcing new equipment and restructured our lunchtime arrangements. Our bid was successful and although it is a very tight timescale we hope to have a new kitchen ready for the start of term in September 2014. Importantly, the additional dining capacity will give our children time to eat.

Future plans

Cookery activities will be offered to small groups of children and we have plans for them to write cookery books based on their experiences in school. The catering team are potentially extending working hours into the evening to prepare take away suppers for parents and cater for community events as well as keeping pace with demand for Celebration Cakes.

Whatever your view of the introduction of this initiative I believe it is a real opportunity for schools to make a difference to the lives of their children and be an important factor in their eventual life success.

9d. The Secondary Experience

Richard Scott, School Business Manager at Plume School, Malden in Essex, describes the school's journey to provision of a successful and well supported catering service.

Context

Plume school is a large 11–18 standalone academy with over 1800 students on two sites a mile apart. It has always been a challenge to make a catering enterprise break even given the need to run two kitchens and provide dining facilities on both sites. The school sites are at either end of the town High Street with the attractions of several fast food outlets only a few steps away.

To further complicate arrangements the kitchen on the smaller site serving years 7 and 8 is in a very old building and has required considerable refurbishment over the years including new floors and removal of asbestos. This site now also accommodates for lunch the 100 or more pupils from the adjacent primary school who are eligible for free school meals or who pay for a hot meal.

On the larger site the kitchen is a designated District emergency and training facility and is thus larger than would be normal for a school of 1200 students. While this might sound attractive it means that we have limited opportunity to remodel and make better use of space to improve the dining area.

Previous experience

The objective of a year-end 'break even' financial position was previously difficult to sustain. Also, over the years governors tried a variety of catering providers including 'outsourcing' to different commercial enterprises and employing an 'in-house' team. In spite of glossy brochures and confident assertions that they can make catering pay, the commercial companies were not any more successful than an 'in-house' team in achieving a sustainable financial position let alone a consistent profit.

Two key elements contributed to this: the number of staff needed to run two kitchens and ineffective stock control. Included in the latter is the need to manage expectations especially of the older students in terms of what is on offer.

Governing body decisions

A few years ago governors made it a priority to work with students and staff to encourage healthy eating, improve student dining experiences and manage purchasing and costings to develop a commercially viable service. It was agreed to restructure the catering staff and employ a commercially minded catering manager at a commensurate salary in order to provide students with nutritionally appropriate food, at outlets where they could 'grab and go' or sit and chat if they wished and at competitive prices. This coupled with a 'no exit' policy, better communication with parents about what was on offer including the nutritional value and allergy information (parents can check exactly what their son or daughter has eaten during the week) and cashless catering has had a huge impact.

Governors agreed that a capital investment should underpin the strategy to make 'dining in' the preferred option of students and staff. We invested in equipment and additional dining facilities including an 'Italian' style outlet as part of a general purpose hall and a dedicated sixth form college coffee shop with proper coffee equipment on the larger site. Picnic tables have also been provided to increase dining space in good weather.

The smaller site has a much improved kitchen and dining facility and although it offers a more limited menu it is targeted towards preferences of the students with a focus on healthy eating. Picnic tables are provided in a sheltered shady quad area. The introduction of a cashless catering system has ensured a quick flow through of students so there is a minimal amount of time spent queuing and the nutritional and option choice information available to parents has been well received.

Food and drink is available before school, at break and lunch times and more flexibly for the sixth form college students. Currently we provide over 200 free school meals and approximately 750 other meals during the day.

My role as SBM

I had overall responsibility for the implementation of the capital projects agreed and focus now on ensuring that there is a year-on-year balanced budget or better.

To do this effectively I undertake thorough and regular monitoring of the financial aspects of the catering facility and the monthly production of a trading profit and loss account which is a crucial tool in identifying trends in the department such as increasing consumable costs, adjustments in staffing and any reduction in income.

A core element of the profit and loss monitoring is a robust approach to stock levels and values. In addition to the financial aspects of stock control in catering, getting a firm grip on stock requirements has proved essential in ensuring wastage is reduced to a minimum. The implementation of daily wastage sheets, to record any disposal of food or ingredients, and an understanding of what already exists has had a dramatic effect on making staff recognise the need to make best use of resources.

Value for money and best value are phases often banded around schools when discussing procurement; however this is also true for the catering department, where complacency can arise in suppliers. Huge savings have been made at the school from regularly testing the market to ensure that prices remain competitive. To this end, we have reduced administration costs by reducing the vast number of different suppliers that the school uses. Not only has this produced efficiency in administration and ordering, but has generated better prices from the economies of scale that we are now able to offer.

In order to make all of the above work there must be clear lines of communication at all levels, from the SBM through the Catering Manager down to the food service assistants in order for everyone to be aware of what is trying to be achieved. I meet daily with the Catering Manager to discuss prices, sales activity and staffing. These regular but brief meetings, identify emerging trends, enable us to nip any problems 'in the bud' before they have taken hold as well as respond quickly to expand positive feedback and engage student interest and loyalty. The ability of our Catering Manager is a crucial factor in achieving this outcome and has been the single most effective element of our approach to catering.

This communication also must continue upwards, with regular (termly) dialogue to the school SLT and governors. This helps maintain an understanding from everyone of the value of school catering and assists when planning longer-term strategic direction of the catering service such as improving the quality of ingredients, expanding the ranges of food on offer and planning future building and resourcing requirements. The SBM role is pivotal in this providing oversight of both the educational aspirations and economic realities of the school.

And finally...

There was no 'quick fix'. The implementation of a coherent catering strategy took some time and not inconsiderable budget demands. Nearly two years later we are noticing the impact on student awareness of healthy eating and the enhancement of school ethos and feel that it has been well worth the effort. Perhaps the following two examples demonstrate this:

- A governor welcomed the format of the catering updates as being brief, notably positive in terms of financial position and strategic in terms of forward planning rather than the former experience of problems in these areas
- A student eulogising about the chocolate brownie asked the Catering Manager how to make it and was quite 'unfazed' when told that a key ingredient was beetroot.

9e. Top Tips for Managing Catering

1. Refer to Section 1 of our Effective Governance guide which explains the role of governors in determining the strategic direction of the school. This is important given the introduction of Universal Free School Meals for KS1
2. Have a clear vision for the catering service at your school
3. Involve governors in creating the vision and planning the implementation
4. Undertake regular communication and surveys with pupils and parents to ensure maximum use of the service. This helps to keep the service viable
5. Ensure that the person who is in charge of the catering service (catering manager) has access to the relevant training and support especially with the introduction of the new food standards
6. Ensure that the catering manager has clear lines of accountability and communication. Regular but brief meetings with the SBM to report on the financial situation will help to ensure a balanced budget and enable a quick response to market prices, weather factors or pupil needs
7. Governors need to keep the finances of catering under review. For schools with Infant provision there needs to be a thorough overview of meals provided and finances claimed
8. Explore how working with other schools may bring benefits in purchasing, training and food preparation
9. Think about innovative ways in which the catering service might be able to increase volume, diversify activity and increase profitability
10. Keep an eye on sources of advice and support as this will help develop thinking about your catering service

Chapter 10

Practicalities Of Conversion For The School Business Manager

10a. Introduction

This chapter looks at the role of the School Business Manager during conversion and offers some practical hints for undertaking the role.

Focus of the chapter

Schools considering converting to Academy Status have many issues to think about. This chapter outlines some of these and intends to give School Business Managers the confidence to consider conversion and introduce them to sources of guidance and support.

The key questions a School Business Manager should think about and governors should ask are:

- Are governors aware of the difference between being a maintained school and being an academy?
- Is the school leadership and the Governing Body prepared for increased responsibility and increased autonomy?
- Is the SBM and the finance team ready to meet the demands of being an independent not-for-profit company operating under Company Law and the Charities Commission?
- Has the school set up banking arrangements?
- Is the Management Information System suitable for an academy?
- Has time been allowed for the SBM and governors to handle the application for conversion?
- Who will provide legal support? (FASNA members are entitled to 10% reduction in fees from Stone King)
- Has the school attended any of the FASNA events on academy conversion?

Overview

The Government has recognised that for many primary converters their current staffing structure is unlikely to include an experienced SBM. For this reason at the time of going to press, there are additional grants available to any group of three or more primaries entering into a Multi-Academy Trust structure. This money reflects the need to have good business skills available to the new academy and is intended to provide support for the schools during the conversion process as well. The clear implication is that once the Multi-Academy Trust is established the schools will merge back office functions and share this key role.

Funding Overview

There are some important differences between the financial status of a maintained school and an academy especially if the school is not currently a cheque book holding school. Funding is replicated on the Local Authority scheme but comes from the Education Funding Agency (EFA) on a monthly basis with a slight frontload for the first month of conversion to assist a smooth cash flow. Pupil premium and SEN money comes from the Local Authority.

The financial year runs from 1st September to 31st August and the final report and accounts of the academy must be audited and deposited with DfE and Companies House by 31st December.

A bank account in the name of the Academy Trust must be open on the first day of conversion so that the first tranche of funding from the EFA can be transferred. Depending on the month of conversion the first set of accounts may cover more than the financial year.

VAT is recoverable in arrears every three months. If the school has a nursery, uniform shop or other trading activity which generates over a specified income it may be necessary to set up a separate trading company for these activities.

Role of the School Business Manager during conversion

It is often the case that the SBM project manages the conversion because the majority of the tasks are related to finance and usually to additional responsibilities to the role of the SBM. There will also be the need to ensure that the timeline for conversion and completion of the legal documentation is managed.

Governors are the decision makers and should therefore be well informed throughout the process and understand the implications of decisions they make. It makes sense for the SBM to work closely with the governor who is leading the conversion process and the Headteacher to ensure a consistent flow of communication and timely progress.

Governors should be encouraged to undertake a skills audit to evidence their fitness for an enhanced financial scrutiny and monitoring role. New appointments should be made to strengthen this area if necessary. If the new academy will breach the financial limits for a separate audit committee this should also be established by governors.

Once the Academy Order has been signed and the school has access to the £25,000 grant for legal and other expenses, which is available to every individual school, the SBM may be charged with identifying an appropriate legal advisor and acting as the main school contact.

During the conversion period it is useful for the SBM to undertake some appropriate training focused on the role in an academy. You will also need to understand the principles of TUPE transfer and HR matters.

Finance related tasks prior to conversion

- If the school is not a cheque book school you will need to discuss closure of the bank account with the LA as soon as practical. The LA does not have the power to retain any funds but it does have a period of time in which to agree with the school the closing balance and get that transferred to the new bank account

- It is important that a new bank account is open and operational from day one of conversion. Even if the school already has a bank account and is not changing the name, a new bank account must be opened
- Another key decision is pay roll provider. Many new academies stay with the LA if they will offer this service. It is worth seeking quotes from commercial providers but you will need to identify their understanding of the educational context and assess their ability to complete pension returns and payments. There is no requirement to move pay roll provision from the LA on conversion
- Insurance policies in the name of the academy must be in place from midnight plus one minute of the day of conversion. The SBM will probably be charged with seeking quotes from current providers including the LA from which the governors will make a decision. As the number of academies grows so this is becoming a commercially competitive area
- As preparation for conversion the SBM may have to assess the readiness of the school's financial IT system and staffing structure and make recommendations for changes where appropriate. Arrangements for auditors, financial support and Responsible Officer may need to be investigated and discussed with governors

Finance related tasks post conversion

- Register with HMRC as the PAYE number will change
- Register for Corporation Tax
- Register with Companies House
- Change name on licences
- Inform relevant suppliers and businesses of change of status
- Remember that the financial year is the same as the academic year for budget setting and monitoring purposes but that the fiscal year is still operative for pension contributions and returns

The first task of the SBM post conversion will usually be to work with the governors' Finance Committee and Headteacher to agree an indicative budget and approve appointment of both the Responsible Officer and the auditors (**see chapter 4 on Auditors**). The Accounting Officer is ex-officio the Headteacher as he/she is the person ultimately responsible in the school, for the financial management.

The SBM will usually be responsible for the preparation of the accounts for the end of the financial year and will need to ensure that they have gone through the correct process as regards governor approval and audit so that they can be lodged with Companies House and DfE by 31st December.

One of our case studies here describes in a very comprehensive and practical way, the responsibilities of the academy in respect of ensuring correct and timely pension contribution and information for the staff.

10b. A Primary School Perspective

Rachel Ward, Executive Business Manager of Tall Oaks Academy Trust, Gainsborough, Lincolnshire, offers advice and encouragement if you are starting the conversion journey.

Things I wish I'd known – Top tips for the conversion

My top tips for survival are:

- **Expect the unexpected and be flexible**
  The academy conversion process can seem very lonely for the SBM as the rest of school life carries on at the normal pace. It is behind the scenes where all the work is taking place and it won't all go smoothly.

- **Don't forget to communicate**
  You will be juggling a number of tasks and needing to communicate with a range of people. Governors need to understand that there will be additional meetings as the conversion process proceeds and that they will have some important decisions to make. Their role and way of working may need to change after conversion to fit in with a different financial year and ensure they recognise their role in accountability for financial probity and school progress.

- **Always ask for help**
  Find somebody who has successfully managed the process and use their experience and expertise to prompt you, guide you through the minefield and reassure you that you are doing the right thing. FASNA will help you here and put you in touch with another school which will provide support.

- **Download an academy implementation pack**
  This is available from the internet and tick off tasks as you complete them. This will remind you of things you still need to do, and, more importantly, show you light at the end of the tunnel when it seems you are getting nowhere. Ensure key governors and the Headteacher are informed about the range of tasks and identify where they need to take decisions or actions.

- **Ensure the school has procured the services of experienced professionals**
  As SBM you will probably be the main contact with the legal advisor, accountants etc. and you need to have confidence that they understand the educational environment and have experience of academy conversion. This will help to smooth any 'glitches' encountered on the way and keep the conversion process on track and on time as far as possible.

- **Share the load**
  It is impossible to convert an academy and continue to perform your everyday duties. These should be delegated to other staff and temporary staff engaged if necessary as soon as the decision to proceed with the conversion is agreed. You need time to think, time to plan and time to make things happen. It is very likely that additional finance staff will need to be appointed after conversion and this should be planned into the budget.

- **Use your conversion grant wisely**

  If one of your new/existing providers can take some of the workload from you for a negotiated fee, then let them. We used our HR advisor to carry out some of the TUPE work.

- **Consider best value at all times**

  This is particularly important when procuring suppliers and services for the new Academy. The difference in service charges quoted by companies can vary considerably. Always ask for a Service Level Agreement or, at the very least, a concise breakdown of what you can expect to receive as part of the procured service as this can also vary widely.

- **Be open to change**

  The change to the financial year and accounting practices mean that you will need to change many of the school's existing systems including the IT provision and procedures. My role has changed beyond imagination. Being an Academy Business Manager is a completely different role to a Local Authority School Finance Manager. Whilst I am able to call on my previous experiences to carry out my role efficiently, I am now required to work at a completely new level. I have had to take a back seat from school life and take on a more strategic, focussed role to ensure that the Academy continues to thrive and meets its legal obligations whilst remaining an outstanding education provider.

- **Professional development**

  As an important part of the conversion process consider your own professional development to enable you to meet the challenges of your enhanced role. Undertake relevant training before the conversion process starts if possible. Understanding the demands of a different accounting system linked to a different financial year will help you to plan your annual cycle of activities effectively.

10c. Teacher and Support Staff Pensions

Corrina Beckett, Finance and Business Director at Barnby Road Academy in Newark, Nottinghamshire, takes the mystique out of this process for the School Business Manager in an academy which does not buy the service from their payroll provider.

How to administer staff pensions was one of the main worries that I had when we converted to academy status in September 2010. I have been administering the pensions at our Academy for over three years now and I hope that this chapter will help alleviate any worries that you may have if, like Barnby Road, this service is managed 'in-house'.

Pension administration is a question of knowing what you need to do and when you need to do it. On conversion to an academy the financial year follows the academic year but the pensions year still complies with the traditional financial year ending on 31st March.

In the academy structure the Academy Trust is the employer and unless the academy has a pay roll provider who takes on the pension administration it will almost certainly be up to the SBM to undertake all the practical functions of the employer relating to pay and pensions. In any event, the ultimate responsibility for ensuring staff pensions are administered correctly remains with the employer so it is good practice for the SBM to have some understanding of the process.

There are three types of pensions and you will need to administer and register with the appropriate body:

1. Teachers' Pensions
2. Local Government Pension Scheme (LGPS)
3. Additional Voluntary Contributions (AVCs)

1. Teachers' Pensions

This is a national scheme run by the Teachers' Pensions and once you have converted to academy status there are no changes to the employer contribution rate and it is a seamless transition.

You will need to contact Teachers' Pensions prior to conversion to register as the employer with them. To complete registration you need to send an e-mail to academies@teacherpensions.co.uk with the following information:

Your full name

- Your job role
- E-mail and telephone contact details
- Academy name (and details of any Academy Trust or Umbrella Trust you are part of)
- Date of conversion (if known)
- The Local Authority your Academy is situated in

Once Teachers' Pensions has all this information you will be registered and receive an email detailing your responsibilities and giving information about help and support should you require it.

The e-mail will also include a registration form for the 'Employer Portal' which is a secure transfer utility and allows both Teachers' Pension and the Academy SBM to send and receive data securely.

Your Local Authority will complete a TR8 (Leaver form) for all the teaching staff within the pension scheme and you, as the new employer, will need to complete a TR6 (Notification of Teacher Appointment form) for all your teaching staff. The TR6 can be found at: www. teacherpensions.co.uk/formsandfactsheets

You will need to complete and submit the 'monthly breakdown contributions payment slip' to Teachers' Pension by the 7th of the following month after your payroll (i.e. January payroll contributions need to be paid by the 7th February). The monthly contributions breakdown form is very easy to complete, once you have entered the contributory salary, there are ratio checks to tell you whether you have paid the right amounts for both the employers and the teachers' contributions.

Once this form has been completed you will need to upload the form using the Employer portal and then ensure that your payment is received by the 7th of the following month at Teachers' Pensions. There is a financial penalty if payment is late (you are allowed one or two months' grace, as a new employer, but after that it is £25 for every payment that is received late).

You will need to agree with your payroll provider as to whether you complete this form or whether they will complete it on your behalf. Either way, do not forget that the Academy Trust is the Employer and usually the SBM will therefore have responsibility for ensuring that the deductions from employees and payments to Teachers' Pension are correct and paid on time.

At the end of the fiscal financial year (31st March) you will need to complete an annual service return. This is a return that lists all the teachers who are employed at your school, or have been used on supply during the year and identifies the salary that they have received for the year and the pension contributions that have made. Again, dependant on your payroll provider, either they will provide you with this information, or if you run payroll 'in-house' you will have these figures on your system. These figures are then transferred to the annual service return that can be downloaded from the employer portal.

I have found the Teachers' Pension website very easy to use and full of excellent guidance notes and resources and, as a further support, Teachers' Pension also provide/allocate a dedicated 'Employer Relationship Manager' to give you advice whenever needed. There are also excellent training courses available for new academies.

2. Local Government Pension Scheme (LGPS)

The LGPS is the pension scheme for all your support staff in the school and is not one scheme but a number of different regional schemes loosely based on Local Authority areas. Although the contribution rate paid by employee members is applied on a national scale the employer rate varies from scheme to scheme. **All of these schemes are in deficit**.

On conversion to an academy the Academy Trust becomes an approved member of the LGPS and the details of all the members of support staff that are registered and members of the LGPS must be sent to the Actuary. The Actuary will calculate the proportion of your academy 'pension pot' in relation to the whole LGPS 'pension pot'. This acts as your registration to the LGPS for the academy. You need to be aware that there is a financial charge for this which can be allocated to the support grant from the DfE.

It is this calculation that will determine your 'Employer Rate' for contributions as an academy. It could be that your employer rate could be increased, decreased or, as is usually the case, remain the same. One aspect of the actuarial calculation is that the portion of the LGPS deficit appropriate for your staff (depending on number and demographic distribution) is identified as an actual amount. The annual actuarial valuation report will identify this sum which has to be included in your final accounts. To put this figure into 'layman's terms' it is really the same as having a mortgage. The employer contribution rate, just like a repayment mortgage, includes a percentage for paying off an appropriate potion of the deficit over 20 years. All schools will pay this but until you convert to academy status the portion applicable to a particular school is not identified.

Unlike Teachers' Pensions scheme, there are no 'leaver forms' or 'new starter forms' to be completed on conversion.

The monthly administration of the LGPS is very similar to the Teachers' Pensions scheme. A monthly payment slip has to be completed which is simply the total employees' contribution for the month and the total employer's contribution for the month. This has to be returned to the Local Authority's Pension department along with the payment by the 15th of the following month after payroll.

Dependant on your payroll provider, you will be provided with these figures or will have them if you are processing payroll in-house and again you need to adhere to the payment deadline.

At the end of the fiscal year there is an annual return to be completed (PEN57 – this is the Nottinghamshire LA form and other LAs may have a different form) which is called a 'Final Statement of Contributions Paid'. These figures are the total figures of all amounts paid over the year.

Additional to the PEN57, there is another return that needs to be completed prior to the end of your financial year. This return (FRS17) is required for your Company accounts to be produced and is a return that is sent to the Actuary. It requires your employee and employer contributions for the academic year, the total pensionable pay and also the estimated pensionable pay for the following **academic** year. There will be a charge for this return and consequent valuation report, so you will need to allow for this in your budget on an annual basis.

The LGPS at Nottinghamshire Local Authority has an excellent team and website that are available for everyday queries and questions. They also run training courses for new academies and also 'end-of-year' seminars for both 'new and old' converters.

3. Additional Voluntary Contributions (AVCs)

These are voluntary additional pension contributions made by staff into a scheme run independently of the main Teachers' Pensions or LGPS schemes. You may find that your academy does not have any member of staff currently paying into one or other of these schemes but it is advisable to check whether there are any new members of these schemes on a regular basis.

There are two AVC companies that I have registered with:

1. **Prudential**
2. **Scottish Widows**

Prudential is the additional contribution provider for teachers. You will need to contact them either by e-mail at avc.admin@prudential.co.uk or by post at AVC Customer Service, Prudential, Stirling FK9 4UE. The form to complete monthly is straight forward, you simply enter the teacher's name, their National Insurance number and the amount they have contributed and simply post to Prudential by the following 15th of the month after payroll.

Scottish Widows is the additional contribution provider for support staff. Again, you will need to contact them at Scottish Widows, PO Box 902, 15 Dalkeith Road, Edinburgh, EH16 5BU. There is no official paying-in slip to complete, you will need to send the information of any payments on letter-headed paper, along with the payment by the following 15th of the month after payroll.

The easiest way to remember all the payments dates is to produce a tick list for each month such as the example below:

December 2013 Payroll

Payee	Amount £	Date sent
Teacher Pension	3957.00	01/01/2014
LGPS	3000.00	10/01/2014
Prudential	200.00	10/01/2014
Scottish Widows	50.00	10/01/2014

I hope that this short explanation of pensions has helped to dispel some of the myths and given you the confidence to feel that you will manage the payments efficiently.

10d. Top Tips for the Practicalities of Conversion

Provided by Rachel Ward, Executive Business Manager of Tall Oaks Academy Trust

During the first year I found it helpful to:

1. Refer governors to Section 6 of the FASNA Effective Governance guide to enable them to understand their responsibilities in conversion and beyond
2. Plan an annual cycle for review of policies and procedures, especially for the first year after conversion
3. Have regular meetings with the Headteacher to review plans and progress
4. Ensure meetings of the Directors/Governors are programmed to fit in with the reporting cycle
5. Prepare routine financial reports for the Finance Committee and the Accounting Officer and ensure stringent checks and balances are in place to provide transparency and a clear understanding of the accounts by all parties
6. Monitor the Risk Register to ensure all targets are implemented and met
7. Monitor and maintain the Management Information Systems in preparation for the Census and accounting reports
8. Review the mid-term and long-term financial plan with the Finance Committee to ensure the Academy is maintaining its strategic direction. Be prepared to up-date it regularly as additional costs will be incurred for services previously 'free' from the Local Authority
9. Subscribe to the EFA Bulletin. This will give you the up-to-date essential information you need to meet financial deadlines, comply with changes to legislation and alert you to forthcoming EFA requirements so that you continue to comply with your Funding Agreement and Articles
10. Take every opportunity to network with colleagues in a similar role or from a similar setting and keep up to date with training opportunities
11. The Trust joined FASNA which has provided us with an avenue for enquiry and training opportunities specific to our requirements. We have also attended the Academies Shows, courses supported by NASBM and Westminster briefings
12. Be prepared to travel to London as this is where most of the important training and briefing sessions take place. This applies to teaching staff as well, as there are specific academy-focused opportunities which are not usually available locally. Travel expenses need to be budgeted for

School Business Manager As Clerk To Governors And Company Secretary

11a. Introduction

This chapter explores the trend for the School Business Manager to take on the role of clerk to governors and/or company secretary

> **Focus of the chapter**
>
> This chapter will enable the school business manager to understand the key elements of the additional roles and the need for clarity about role boundaries and potential areas for conflict of interest. Governors also need to be clear about their role and responsibilities in appointing the clerk and company secretary and ensuring the role is undertaken effectively.
>
> **Key questions a business manager should think about and governors should ask are:**
>
> 1. Do governors and the SBM fully understand the increasing importance placed on the role of clerk to governors?
> 2. Is there a clear job description for the additional role(s)?
> 3. Are line management responsibilities and annual reviews for any additional role clear?
> 4. Does the SBM have the appropriate expertise to undertake the role, including desirable interpersonal skills ?
> 5. What might be the impact of the additional responsibilities on the substantive role as SBM?
> 6. How will the meeting cycle for the governing body or academy trust 'fit' with the financial cycle in terms of 'pinch points'?
> 7. What support or professional development is needed for the SBM to undertake all roles?

Context

With many schools and academies using their School Business Manager as Clerk to the Governors and / or Company Secretary, this chapter looks at the differences between these roles, the demands of the roles and the skills required to carry them out successfully. Obviously, this dual role (which may be combined with yet other roles as outlined in other chapters) will require a great deal from the SBM and needs to be properly monitored by the Governors.

Whether or not a combined role encompassing these functions would work depends entirely on the school in question.

Schools should seriously consider the impact of combining these positions. If the roles are combined it is important to have a clear line of accountability for each element of the role and to ensure that the SBM has sufficient time for each element of their role. As has been pointed out elsewhere in this guide there is a danger of delegating too many responsibilities to the SBM! This is particularly so where a school has a large number of committees and the Clerk to Governors is required to administer and minute the activities of all those committees as well as the main Board of Directors ('the Governing Body') in a single academy trust.

If the roles are to be combined, the SBM needs to prepare by familiarising themselves with their academy trust's Articles of Association. They should already be familiar with the funding agreement and the Academies' Financial Handbook. Governors and Headteachers should ensure that the SBM has a clearly defined job description, a performance management structure that encompasses all aspects of their role with explicit targets and support.

For governors and Headteachers / Principals, this chapter sets out to advise on how to manage this situation and gives some case studies of how this is being done in other schools.

11b. The School Business Manager as Clerk to Governors – A Secondary Perspective

This chapter looks at the additional role of Clerk to Governors, which the School Business Manager might be asked to undertake.

Roy Blackwell, Clerk to the United Westminster Schools Foundation, explains the tensions in the dual role and offers some good practice suggestions.

The Job Description

The Clerk should be appointed by the governing body and, if the role is an existing element of the SBM job description, the governing body should regularly confirm that they are content with the arrangement. The Clerk is accountable to the governing body and needs to work effectively with the Chair of Governors, the Headteacher and other governors. Good communication and interpersonal skills are a prime requisite of this dual role and the robust observation of confidentiality boundaries.

An important element of the role is to advise the governing body on constitutional matters, duties and powers and ensure they work within the appropriate legislative framework. This means that the Clerk must keep up to date with governance issues and the accountability requirements of an academy.

The key operational tasks of the Clerk are listed below.

Organisational tasks

In terms of governing body meetings the Clerk to Governors will:

- Work effectively with the Chair and Headteacher before the governing body meeting to prepare an agenda
- Ensure all agenda papers are produced on time for circulation with the agenda
- Comply with relevant timelines for circulating meeting papers, usually seven days but some Articles of Association for academies have fourteen-day notice periods
- Circulate the draft agenda to the Chair and Headteacher for approval
- Record the attendance of governors at the meeting
- Advise the governing body on effective governance and procedural matters where necessary before, during and after the meeting
- Record discussions as evidence that the governors are being both supportive and challenging to the Headteacher
- Record all decisions accurately and objectively and identify who is responsible for any agreed action
- Send draft minutes as soon as possible to the Chair and Headteacher for amendment and approval
- Circulate the approved draft minutes along with the agenda for the next meeting
- Act as Chair for that part of the meeting at which the Chair is elected

In terms of membership the Clerk to Governors will:

- Maintain copies of current terms of reference and membership of committees and working parties and nominated liaison or special governors

- Advise governors and appointing bodies of the expiry of the term of office before the term expires so elections or appointments may be organised in a timely manner
- Inform the governing body of any changes to its membership through external appointments
- Maintain governor meeting attendance records and advise the governing body of non-attendance of governors
- Ensure the declaration of business interests forms are completed annually
- Ensure that 'Declaration of business interests' is on all agendas
- Ensure that the Disclosure and Barring Service (DBS) checks are completed for governors when appropriate

Advice and information

There is an increasing focus on the role of Clerk as the independent key advisor and support to the governing body. This means that the Clerk needs to keep up to date with governance and educational changes and be an effective link between the school and the governors.

It is important that the Clerk has access to legal advice in order to advise the governing body on procedural matters particularly if a governor panel is hearing an appeal or exclusion review. As the role of Clerk is being scrutinised more closely it is becoming accepted as good practice that the Clerk should also clerk all governing body committees so as to provide a consistent approach and efficient service to governors.

The Clerk should be prepared to assist with elections to the governing body if necessary and give advice and support to new governors and those taking on a new role such as Chair, Vice Chair or Chair of Committee. Part of this responsibility includes the need to ensure that there is a 'Governor Handbook' comprising documents such as the Articles of Association if an academy, the current structure and meeting cycle, terms of reference for main committees, any code of conduct or similar document and information about the school. This list is not exhaustive and governors should be encouraged to make the handbook 'their own' reflecting the core values of the school and their expectations of all governors for commitment, participation and professionalism.

Good practice for effective clerking

It goes without saying that a core function of the Clerk is to maintain scrupulous records including copies of statutory policies and others approved by the governing body noting the date of approval and next review.

The relationship between the Clerk and the Chair is crucial in setting the tone and conduct of the meeting. Careful planning and a common understanding of how the meeting will be run identifying any potentially difficult agenda items or those which will require some more detailed consideration will help to keep the meeting focused.

I believe it is important for the agenda to give an idea of the time allocated to each item which will enable you as Clerk to 'nudge' the Chair if timings are slipping.

Be prepared to advise the Chair if you feel a discussion is straying into difficult territory especially if, for example, a parent is raising a personal issue or there is a detailed discussion about a named member of staff. You need to determine a protocol for this with the Chair. I would suggest you encourage the Chair to ask you a question along the lines of: "Are we in danger of crossing protocol boundaries if we pursue the discussion in this way?" This gives you as Clerk the opportunity to say that your advice is to curtail the discussion or continue to consider the principle involved without reference to particular staff or members. By such means a potentially difficult situation can be diffused without the Chair seeming to have exerted unreasonable control.

Just as you will ensure papers are distributed before the meeting, so should others. Try to persuade governors and others not to 'table' papers and if they do persuade the Chair to defer detailed discussion on the paper until the next meeting. This will help to dissuade the 'tabling' habit.

Likewise, try to persuade the Chair to avoid allowing someone to read through a document she/he is presenting (governors have already done that). The Chair could introduce the item by saying something like: "Thank you for the paper which we have all read; can you highlight two or three key points and then I will ask governors if they have any questions to put to you".

It might be useful to offer templates for reports/papers etc. For example, it might be helpful for every report to have a standard heading and clear recommendations at its conclusion.

Governors may also need reminding from time to time about the confidentiality of governors meeting and the need to abide by majority decisions. Prompt the Chair to emphasise this periodically.

The SBM or Bursar will need to be ready to talk through any financial reports etc on the agenda. You cannot speak as SBM and Clerk at the same time, so this needs to be very carefully managed and is a good argument for having a separate note taker. The Chair could emphasise your dual role by making it clear that in the ensuing discussion you are reporting as the SBM and you could make it clear that in offering advice on procedure for example you are doing so in your capacity as Clerk. This will help to avoid situations which might attract allegations of conflict of interest.

To pursue the 'conflict of interest' concern, a good example of where you might have to withdraw from your role of Clerk is if, for example, there is a staff discipline hearing. In this instance it would be good practice to have someone else undertake not just the minute taking at the hearing but the selection of a governor panel and all administrative tasks in including offering appropriate advice. In these days of an ever more litigious society the cost of external legal clerk in this instance may well be a best value option.

The other obvious area where there needs to be a clear distinction is in the appointment of the Headteacher and senior staff. You should not be directly involved in the appointment of your line manager nor should you be directly involved in the appointment of your successor, so there will be certain functions of the Clerk's role that you will not be able to carry out, e.g. being present at interviews, helping to draw up job descriptions.

Finally, the Clerk is not just a minute-taker (in fact that could be delegated to someone else for the main governing body meeting). It is the advisory role that is of the utmost importance and governors need to feel they can trust you to keep them on the 'straight and narrow'.

And finally...

The SBM acting as Clerk to Governors can be a cost effective and time efficient way of providing appropriate support and guidance to the governing body.

None of the above problems are impossible to solve, but you will need to go through the implications of being the Clerk very carefully with the Headteacher and governors so that there are agreed arrangements in place for those moments when there might be a 'conflict of interests for you'. This is as much for your welfare as for the good of the governing body.

11c. Combining the Role of Company Secretary and Clerk of the Governors

Myles Taaffe from Stone King LLP describes the differences between the role of Company Secretary and Clerk to Governors.

Whether it's a meeting of the trustees of Barnardo's, the shareholders of Virgin Atlantic or the governors of a school, an organisation's board meetings should be facilitated by a skilled and organised individual. While Virgin Atlantic no doubt employ a professional Company Secretary to fulfil this function, a school will often expect the Clerk to Governors to take on the additional role when the school converts to academy status. In many cases, this person will be the School Business Manager and it is important that all parties, including the governors, understand the different demands of each role and the boundaries of responsibility.

The difference between a Clerk to Governors and a Company Secretary

The Clerk to Governors has been a vital part of the governance structure of maintained schools for decades and schools will be familiar with the work they do. The role itself is a support function and is, more often than not, focused on three key tasks:

1. Advising governors of procedural and compliance matters
2. Circulating papers before, during and after meetings
3. Taking minutes during meetings

The academies revolution has altered this support function by introducing the concept of a Company Secretary. Academies are operated by the Directors of an academy trust (a private company) and, as with Virgin Atlantic, academy trusts are able (but not obliged) to appoint a Company Secretary.

It can be tempting to think of the Company Secretary as an 'academy-equivalent' to the Clerk to Governors but this would be to misunderstand some fundamental differences. The role of the Company Secretary does include responsibilities usually carried out by the Clerk to Governors but it also includes additional duties arising under company law. In summary the Company Secretary:

1. Must be registered at Companies House
2. Is an officer of the academy trust, with statutory obligations under the Companies Act 2006
3. May be given delegated authority to sign contracts
4. Is responsible for the academy trust's relationship with Companies House

There is no law compelling a private company such as an academy trust to appoint a Company Secretary unless the academy trust's Articles of Association require it.

In the absence of a formal appointment, the legal responsibilities of a Company Secretary will stay with the Directors (the governors in a single academy trust) and in practice the administrative tasks will be delegated to the Clerk to Governors, the SBM or other staff members.

Key elements of each role

Clerk to Governors

- Advise on the procedures for full governors' meetings and committee meetings
- Give notice to governors of the next meeting
- Circulate the reports of the Headteacher and Chair
- Take minutes
- Circulate copies of minutes
- Maintain a record of governors' terms of office
- Circulate information about governor training opportunities
- Demonstrate good organisational skills to assist with record keeping

Company Secretary

- Accurately apply the academy trust's:
  - Articles of Association
  - Funding agreement
  - Local governing body terms of reference (where applicable)
- Understand the implications of the Companies Act for the academy trust
- Differentiate between members and directors/ governors/trustees
- Demonstrate a good working knowledge of directors' statutory duties
- Demonstrate good organisational skills to assist with record keeping and prompt statutory filings
- Maintain the formal registers in the company books

Are the roles mutually exclusive?

The functions of the Clerk to Governors will always be needed. The question is should the additional functions of the Company Secretary be added to the Clerk to Governors job description or, alternatively, should a separate person be appointed to carry out these functions? The answer will depend on practicalities and the available resources of each academy trust; either solution is appropriate.

As the Company Secretary will still need to ensure that minutes of Directors' meetings are taken and kept in the company records, whoever undertakes the Company Secretary role (if separate) will have to supervise the work of the Clerk to Governors to an extent. There is therefore an advantage in combining the roles if possible.

An alternative structure would be to split the roles between two individuals each being accountable to the governors separately. Here the Clerk to Governors would continue to support the governors in the same way as they have done historically with the Company Secretary carrying out additional oversight regarding minutes produced by the Clerk. If adopting this structure, it is important to ensure the split of responsibilities is clearly documented.

In a Multi Academy Trust the separation of the Clerk to Governors and the Company Secretary roles can be much clearer. The Company Secretary would usually provide the support to the Board of Directors whereas the school Clerk would support the local governing body and/or advisory board of each academy.

Can the roles of School Business Manager, Company Secretary and Clerk to Governors be combined in practice?

Whether or not a combined role encompassing all three functions would work depends entirely on the dynamics of the school in question.

In combining the roles it is important to have an unambiguous line of accountability for each element and also identify a framework of operation which allows the SBM the time to carry out their primary function.

Schools should seriously consider the impact of rolling all three positions into one: in particular whether the SBM has the time to carry out all the clerking and company secretary tasks effectively. This is particularly so where a school has a large number of committees and the Clerk to Governors is required to administer and minute the activities of all those committees as well as the main Board of Directors ('the Governing Body') in a single academy trust.

Preparing for the additional roles

One of the most important ways that a SBM should prepare for the additional roles is by familiarising themselves with their academy trust's Articles of Association and funding agreement as well as the Academies' Financial Handbook. These documents are to a large extent the 'academy-equivalent' to the constitution regulations which only apply to maintained school governing bodies.

The Articles of Association regulate how the academy trust meetings are conducted and decisions made. Knowledge of the key provisions of the articles is a prime requisite for the effective undertaking of the Company Secretary role; the Companies House website which contains a range of guidance notes and frequently asked question is a useful resource for Company Secretaries.

11d. The School Business Manager as Clerk to Governors – The Key

In this section, contributed by 'The Key', a number of School Business Managers explain the advantages of undertaking the role of Clerk to Governors.

As quality of governance becomes more high profile with the need to have a professional and skilled body of governors who can evidence clearly their impact on school improvement, so the need for professional clerking is becoming more urgent.

The following SBMs were contacted about this additional role:

- Iain Gosling, SBM and Clerk at Our Lady's RC High School, a voluntary aided school in Manchester
- Simon Murphy, SBM at Kingshurst City Technology College, an academy in Birmingham
- Dean Lennard, SBM and Clerk at Little Ridge Primary School, a community school in East Sussex
- Sonia Spooner, SBM and Clerk to committees at Underwood West Primary School in Cheshire

Context

There was no common pattern to the linking of the two roles. Kingshurst had a long-standing tradition of including the clerking role into the job description for the SBM stemming from the school's earlier status as a city technology college. Simon Murphy, the SBM, felt that the school thus developed a more individual approach to governance, which continued when the school converted to an academy in 2008.

Dean Lennard found that the Clerk's role was an 'add on' he was expected to take when he became Finance Manager for the primary school. This can be a common pattern in the primary sector. Sonia Spooner clerks governors' committees which was part of her first role in the school as an admin assistant. Her role has since developed into that of a Finance Manager, but she still continues to clerk governors' committees.

Iain Gosling too found that his role developed from Finance Manager to SBM and governors considered that he was well placed to give them the high level advice and support they needed. The governors see him as someone who can offer clear procedural advice as well as key strategic information about the school.

Advantages of the School Business Manager as Clerk to Governors

For Simon, the SBM's detailed knowledge of where the school is going is a real advantage. He says SBMs working as Clerks can move beyond just overseeing procedure, and can take advantage of their experience to work particularly closely with the Chair and Principal to drive forward the academy's strategy.

For Iain, taking on the role meant he could better act as a link between the School Leadership Team and the governors, and give them the information and background they need to challenge effectively and make well-informed decisions.

He says that as a SBM and member of the SLT, he has an interest in building an effective governing body, and this is something that may not always be present in a Clerk who is working on a more independent basis.

Dean Lennard says that acting as Clerk supports both the governing body and his own role as SBM. One advantage is that it enables him to understand the importance of key decisions made in areas that are normally outside his remit, such as teaching and learning and the curriculum. It helps him to forecast potential budget implications more effectively and have a more strategic overview of where the school is going.

There are also benefits to be found in inducting governors effectively as he is able to meet them easily and ensure they are quickly informed about school priorities and strategies. New governors have been very appreciative of this, feeling that the Clerk is an integral part of the school and clearly knowledgeable.

Practical issues

Not everyone will agree that the Clerk to Governors role should be undertaken by the SBM, or indeed any member of the school staff, feeling that the potential for conflict of interest is a risk. FASNA's view is that where schools are cognisant of this risk and feel that the advantages outweigh the disadvantages they should be able to continue this practice. Costs for external professional clerking are not insignificant which can be an issue for some schools.

The SBM must be mindful of the need to 'wear the right hat' and ensure that appropriate boundaries are observed. Confidentiality is of paramount importance.

All our above SBMs agreed that well developed organisational and administrative skills are central to managing successfully the dual role, particularly at certain times in the school and financial year.

At Little Ridge Primary School Dean stated that the cyclical nature of governing body meetings means that the focus on clerking responsibilities has peaks and troughs when time management and good communication are essential.

At Our Lady's RC High School Iain stated that at busy times, it may mean that other work is put on hold for a short time.

All agree that the most time-consuming element of the Clerk's role is ensuring that all reports and papers needed for a full governing body meeting are obtained from senior staff or from other sources in due time to go out with the agenda. This becomes even more pressured if there are committee meetings in the same couple of weeks or if meetings coincide with the end of the financial year. It is normal practice for the Clerk to meet with the Chair of Governors or Chair of Committee to agree the agenda and other documents needed. Sometimes this may mean the Clerk doing some research to update governors on for example the latest changes to the Ofsted framework.

Simon Murphy from Kingshurst also carries out the role of Company Secretary with all that entails in ensuring the correct returns are completed and filed with the appropriate body at the right time and keeping records up to date with Companies House. For him, this triple faceted role works well, and is a pattern which other large secondary academies have adopted. However, the caveats about conflict of interest, and the need to be scrupulous about the Company Secretary responsibilities, apply and this will not be a solution which suits all circumstances.

Professionalism

A key skill which the SBM must demonstrate, if they are to undertake the role of Clerk to Governors as well, is the ability to establish good interpersonal relationships. The Clerk is the interface between the Headteacher and senior staff, the Chair of Governors, Chairs of Committees and all governors. As such it is sometimes necessary to be assertive, to be clear about what is acceptable practice and what is not and potentially to act as mediator or adjudicator where there is considerable divergence of opinion.

A good Clerk, who has established constructive and professional relationships with all parties, will find that they are able to support the efficient functioning of the governing body and the progress of the school and thoroughly enjoy the additional involvement.

11e. Top Tips when the SBM undertakes the role of Clerk and/or Company Secretary

For the SBM and governors

1. Refer to Section 3.1 of our Effective Governance guide which organisation and management of the governing body to ensure an accountability framework and may be helpful in identifying key elements of the clerking role
2. Ensure there is a clear job description for the additional role(s) agreed by both parties identifying line management of the additional role(s)
3. Ensure that areas of potential 'conflict of interest' are clarified possibly with the Chair of any meeting when discussing the agenda and alternative arrangements for clerking put in place if appropriate
4. The Chair of any meeting should invite the contribution of the SBM for relevant agenda items and ensure this distinction is noted in the minutes
5. Governors need to ensure that they are effective in questioning the SBM with regard to budget allocations and outcomes
6. Chair of Governors, Chairs of Committees and SBMs need to be aware of the relevant documents setting out governance procedures
7. Chair and Headteacher need to ensure that the additional roles do not impact on the ability of the SBM to discharge the substantive role effectively
8. SBM needs to undertake appropriate Clerk and Company Secretary training to ensure that the responsibility to advise the governing body is fulfilled
9. It is good practice to establish a link to a legal helpline or similar for the SBM, or indeed any person undertaking those roles, to access in the role of Clerk and Company Secretary

Chapter 12

'A Year In The Life Of'

12a. Introduction

In this chapter a SBM from a large secondary school and one from a primary school give an overview of their annual cycle of activities.

A core theme running through the case studies in this guide is that the influence and impact of a SBM on school improvement and progress is directly linked to the status of the role within the school as part of the leadership team and with the authority to take certain decisions.

Keeping a firm grasp on monitoring the budget allocations may sometimes put the SBM in the unenviable position of saying 'No' to staff. The simple act of keeping the colour printer in her office and changing the access code on a frequent basis enabled one SBM in a primary school to make sufficient savings over a year to purchase software to support the pupils on the SEN register.

12b. A Year in the Life of a Secondary School Business Manager

Nigel Goodall, Director of Business and Finance, from Nunthorpe Academy explains the key tasks he undertakes each month.

The job of a SBM can be a very trying and isolating one as many academy staff, even at quite senior levels often do not understand the impact that a good (or bad) SBM can have on an academy, its students, staff and other stakeholders.

At the same time, it can also be an extremely rewarding, varied and challenging one. I thrive on the variety of tasks that arrive on my desk on a daily basis. I have, however, been lucky in that I have a Principal and Board of Directors who have always been supportive of me, involving me at the highest strategic level whilst allowing me the space and freedom to make a lot of decisions and changes in the academy.

The following is a summary of my key financial tasks throughout the year. I find the Business Cycle Wall Planner (available from the DfE website) a very useful tool in identifying these tasks and ensuring I complete them at an appropriate point in the year.

www.gov.uk/government/publications/efa-business-cycle

In common with many SBMs, I have a variety of disparate 'additional' responsibilities such as Health & Safety, income generation, HR, etc. The tasks below therefore merely scratch the surface of what the year entails, but may give the newly appointed SBM an insight to the role and may help colleagues to understand what you are doing when you are ensconced in the finance office.

September

The beginning of the academic year, the beginning of the new financial year for the academy and the beginning of the preparation for the previous year-end accounts. This is the start of a busy four months for the SBM until 31st December when the accounts have to be submitted to the EFA and DfE.

It is really important to engage with the auditors early in the process and ensure you are fully conversant with what they require. At the same time the Principal and governors' audit or finance committee must be kept informed and additional meetings programmed in as soon as possible. The EFA has recently introduced the requirement for a separate audit committee for larger academies which trigger a budget allocation of ten million pounds. Some necessary meetings may be dependent on auditor availability, and arranged at short notice, so be sure that governors understand this.

Any revisions to the Academies Financial Handbook come into effect this month, so be mindful that any changes have been incorporated into the school's financial procedures and regulations.

October

If you have a Sixth Form the 16 to 19 bursary fund management information has to be submitted to the EFA in October.

Continue to progress year-end work with the auditors and governors as appropriate: it is important to keep the momentum going here as December will come round all too quickly. The EFA undertakes a funding audit on a small number of academies to ensure that funding is based on accurate student numbers: this is a routine sampling and nothing to be concerned about.

November

Good meetings with the auditors and governors' involvement through their audit committee or finance committee during the past few weeks will ensure that the work on your year-end audited accounts is coming to an end ready for final approval by the Board of Directors. It is important that the Annual Report is at least read and approved by governors before inclusion into the accounts. I think it is good practice to expect governors to contribute to this report. It does not have to be detailed, but is an overview of their activities and impact on the school during the year.

December

Finally, after a lot of angst and hard work, the audited financial statements, auditor's management letter and value for money statement must be submitted. The deadline for submission to the EFA is 31st December.

The EFA announces the Dedicated Schools Grant award and indicative Pupil Premium Grant for the next year.

Remember to relax and enjoy Christmas and the New Year celebrations.

January

This can be quite a busy month in spite of the fact that the year-end accounts have now been finalised.

The Academy Accounts Return should be uploaded by 31st January. Do make sure you have a login to the Deloitte Online Website as this is where you will upload the data.

The academy trust's accounting officer is required to submit the return. Whilst it may seem a duplication of information, having just submitted your financial statements, this return contains slightly different information. The academy trust's financial statements are prepared in accordance with the Charity Statement of Recommended Practice (SORP) whilst the EFA, DFE and the rest of government, prepare financial statements based on international accounts standards. This means that some information required will not appear in the SORP financial statements.

A detailed guidance document is available on the DfE website. The return must be signed off by the accounting officer and the trust's external auditor on the spreadsheet. You can choose to do this yourself or your auditors will be happy to produce it for you – at a cost of course. But remember they still need to sign it off and you need to consider 'best value' in terms of your time.

This month also sees the deadline for the submission of the Academy Capital Maintenance Fund (AMCF). Academies can bid for funding to support expansion projects or building condition issues. The bid process typically opens with notification of the categories in December with bids to be submitted by the end of January. This process requires careful planning and understanding of the criteria. It can be very time consuming and is usually heavily oversubscribed. Do your homework and start planning early. For example, we started putting a potential project together in September undertaking research, drawing up feasibility plans and speaking to project managers. So once the application process went 'live' we were ready to put together an appropriate bid.

February

The EFA will circulate indicative funding allocations to academies. This needs to be scrutinised carefully. If you want to challenge indicative funding factors or student numbers to the EFA a business case submissions must be made to the EFA. Preliminary work on budget for the next financial year can begin.

March

Final funding allocation is notified to the school. The governors should be involved at this stage in ensuring the budget is focused on school strategic priorities. A key unknown at this time is the impact on the potential staff budget allocation of resignations, appointments and student numbers. In terms of budget planning, given that the staffing budget is a high proportion of the overall allocation, I I find it better to err on the side of caution and over rather than under-estimate our needs.

April

For me, the key event in April is the announcement of outcomes for round 1 of the Academies Capital Maintenance Fund (ACMF) bid submissions. As this fund is always hugely oversubscribed, the result often starts with a rejection. If this is the case, you need to undertake a critical review in order to see how your next bid can be changed to increase your chances of success.

If your bid is successful the need to get work done in the summer break means a period of high activity for all those staff involved in the project to finalise the tender process, draw up contracts, select contractors, work with the project manager who is sometimes the school Site Director to ensure everything is ready to go when the holiday period starts.

It is not unusual for capital building works to be done while the school is in session which can pose a number of logistical problems for the SBM to ensure the continued smooth running of the school.

May

A relatively low key month and for me a chance to catch up on items or start the early strategic planning for any new developments. Academies have until the end of May to publish their financial statements from the previous year on their websites, and the Summer School Census has to be completed.

June

The budget setting process begun in March is finalised this month by a presentation to the governing body and their formal approval. The EFA require the budget forecast return to be submitted by the end of the month.

July

The EFA will confirm the level of Pupil Premium Grant for an academy. The grant is paid in four instalments over the year. This is a good time to consider how the grant can support school priorities and particularly how you will ensure that there is a good audit trail identifying activities supported by the grant, the amount allocated and how the school will evidence the impact. Governors have a responsibility to monitor the grant allocation particularly in terms of value for money and they, with the Principal or relevant senior leader, need to be involved in discussions.

July is also the deadline for qualifying academies to submit their round 2 ACMF bids. The outcomes of these bids are confirmed in October. Good Luck!

August

The trend is now for SBMs to be on 52 week contracts. I find August a time to complete those jobs not directly related to financial management, health and safety matters or premises related tasks for example. The opportunity to get ahead for the next year while the school is quiet is also important for me. It is only in this month that I realise just how pressured some of my days are in other months with all the unexpected things which happen, but it is the variety and pace of the job which I enjoy.

And finally...

This is a limited 'snapshot' of a year in the life of an SBM. The best advice that I have is ensure that you have the firm support and backing of your Principal and Board of Directors, keep your colleagues well informed of what you are doing throughout the year, build a good relationship with your accountants, legal advisers and immediate team, and most importantly, as the posters (and mugs and t-shirts and mouse mats etc) say.....

'Keep Calm and Carry On'

12c. A Year in the Life of a Primary School Business Manager

Linda Summers, School Business Manager of Robinswood Primary Academy in Gloucester explains the routine tasks she undertakes on a regular basis throughout the year

Context

Robinswood is a two-form entry primary academy in a suburb of Gloucester. In September 2013 a new primary school 'Waterfalls' was opened as part of the Academy Trust. The SBM operates across both schools.

Routine tasks

Primary schools rarely have a large administration and finance staff so, as a SBM, I have to be responsible for many routine tasks that in a secondary school would be undertaken by other people.

My first jobs on getting into the office in the morning are the usual administration tasks of sorting the post and checking the overnight emails for anything important. It is my responsibility to ensure that these are passed to the appropriate person. Anything relating to pupils or parents is a high priority and I will usually keep a copy for future reference if needed and will also check that the matter is being dealt with in case there is a phone call from the parent.

Employer related tasks

In terms of staffing, I am responsible for keeping all HR correspondence and records, carrying out review meetings for support staff and for keeping up to date with and informing staff about Local Government Pension Scheme matters. Maintenance of the single central record for Disclosure and Barring Service records is an important part of the job.

It is part of my role to monitor staff absences, arrange day-to-day supply cover. Strategically I may be involved in discussions about the potential financial impact of longer-term sickness or maternity leave. Once a solution is agreed, I ensure that all the correct paperwork is prepared relating to an insurance claim and/or a fixed term contract.

I have responsibility for ensuring HR policies relating to support staff are reviewed regularly and approved by governors and that appropriate support staff undertake training on a regular basis especially with regard to fire safety, food hygiene and first aid.

I also ensure that we have enough qualified mini bus drivers, that refresher training is arranged, and all records of usage and service are up to date.

Financial tasks

I maintain responsibility for ensuring that all purchasing documentation is completed according to our procedures and that orders are tracked and checked on receipt. This includes overseeing all catering invoices and monitoring stock checks on a regular basis.

On a daily basis I will reconcile the petty cash account, arrange reimbursement of expenses where necessary and ensure that we do not have large sums of money in school for any length of time by arranging for Securicor to collect cash and take it to the bank. We do have a number of regular lettings which need to be invoiced, and in some cases followed up for payment, and some additional one-off requests which I deal with on an ad-hoc basis. I prepare the BACS run for invoices on a fortnightly basis

We have a pre-school attached which also admits two-year old children and it is my responsibility to apply for and track the use of grant funding, invoice and keep records of parental payments for additional sessions.

Tasks relating to payroll take place on a monthly basis. I will prepare timesheets for any miscellaneous payment or overtime of certain site staff then check the payroll run with our service provider. Any staff payroll queries will come to me in the first instance so it is important that I keep abreast of pension changes for both teachers and support staff and staff pension decisions relating to their individual circumstances.

We have a school credit card which is useful as it can save us money when purchasing certain items from discount suppliers. I have responsibility for monitoring and checking the use of this, and for completing a regular return which is available for inspection by the Responsible Officer or a governor.

Throughout the year I attend Finance Committee meetings when the budget is scrutinised by governors and strategic discussions about medium and longer-term viability take place. Governors will also expect detailed information about the use of the pupil premium and sports fund monies and about the impact on school standards as a result of the strategies supported by these grants. I prepare and submit the in-year Education Funding Agency returns and prepare the final accounts and report for audit.

These meetings are one of the most rewarding aspects of my role as it gives me an input into the future direction of the school and the opportunity to contribute to improvements in premises and other resources.

During the autumn term I liaise with the auditor and the governing body Finance Committee to arrange the timetable for completion of the accounts by the end of December.

Service and utility provision

Fuel costs can be an expensive budget item and I frequently look for ways to reduce this by changing suppliers or by planning for insulation improvements with the governors.

We buy back a number of services from Gloucester County Council and I monitor the effectiveness in terms of cost and provision before recommending continuation of contract.

I need to keep abreast of insurance funding changes and prepare a recommendation for governors about what we should include in our insurance package. Since the academy insurance grant methodology has changed it has been more important to risk assess our insurance needs carefully. For example, some schools may feel that it is not important for them to have a specific flood or terrorist insurance element.

Insurances are reviewed annually and again towards the end of the contract period when we might decide to re-tender. We deal with IT licences on an annual basis and also the MOT, tax and insurance for the mini bus.

And finally...

I like the variety of my job even though some of the tasks might be thought to be rather 'low level' for a School Business Manager. The interactions with almost the whole school staff and frequently the children mean that no two days are alike. Through my attendance at governing body committee and sometimes full board meetings I have a comprehensive knowledge of the school's important priorities and can use this understanding when drafting the budget or reviewing policies, training needs or services.

Glossary of acronyms

ACMF	Academies Capital Maintenance Fund
ADSBM	Advanced Diploma of School Business Management
AVC	Additional Voluntary Contribution
CSBM	Certificate of School Business Management
CFT	Children's Food Trust
COSSH	Control of Substances Hazardous to Health
DBF	Director of Business and Finance
DBS	Disclosure and Barring Service
DfE	Department for Education
DRBCP	Disaster Recovery and Business Continuity Plan
DSBM	Diploma of School Business Management
EFA	Education Funding Agency
FASNA	Freedom and Autonomy for Schools – National Association
FC	Finance Committee
FDF	Financial Directors Forum
FMS	Financial Management System
GB	Governing Body
H&S	Health and Safety
HR	Human Resources
HSE	Health and Safety Executive
LA	Local Authority
LACSEG	Local Authority Central Spend Equivalent Grant
LGPS	Local Government Pension Scheme
MAT	Multi Academy Trust
NASBM	National Association of School Business Managers
NCTL	National College for Teaching and Leadership
PCSE	Priory Community School Enterprises Limited
PPG	Pupil Premium Grant
RDC	Resources Development Committee
RO	Responsible Officer
SAFE	Safeguarding, Facilities and Estates Committee

SBD	School Business Director
SBM	School Business Manager
SBMCF	School Business Managers' Competency Framework
SDP	School Development Plan
SEF	Self-Evaluation Form
SFVS	Schools Financial Value Standard
SLA	Service Level Agreement
SLT	Senior Leadership Team
SORP	Statement of Recommended Practice
UIFSM	Universal Infant Free School Meals

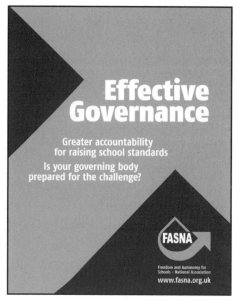

Academy Magazine

Launched in October 2011, Academy celebrates and supports the exciting, fast-growing academy and free school sectors in the UK. Written and read by all those with a professional interest in these state-funded independent schools, the magazine is partnered with FASNA (Freedom and Autonomy for Schools – National Association) and has quickly been recognised as an authoritative voice in the field.

Two-year subscriptions @ £25.00